THE CHILD, SOCIETY AND THE WORLD: UNPUBLISHED SPEECHES AND WRITINGS

D1423633

THE CLIO MONTESSORI SERIES
VOLUME 7

THE CHILD, SOCIETY AND THE WORLD: UNPUBLISHED SPEECHES AND WRITINGS

Maria Montessori
Translated, where necessary, from the original manuscripts by Caroline Juler and Heather Yesson, and with introductory texts by Günter Schulz-Benesch

CLIO PRESS
OXFORD, ENGLAND

This edition has been licensed for publication by the Association Montessori Internationale, Amsterdam. *The Child, Society and the World: Unpublished Speeches and Writings* was first published in German translation under the title *Spannungsfeld Kind-Gesellschaft-Welt. Auf dem Wege zu einer Kosmischen Erziehung* in 1979 (Freiburg, Basel, Vienna: Verlag Herder), compiled and edited by Günter Schulz-Benesch.

British Library Cataloguing in Publication Data
Montessori, Maria, *1870-1952*
   The child, society and the world: unpublished speeches and
   writings – (The Clio Montessori series)
   1. Education. Montessori system
   I. Title
   371.3'92
ISBN 1-85109-112-2

ABC-Clio Ltd.,
Old Clarendon Ironworks,
35a Great Clarendon Street,
OXFORD OX2 6AT, ENGLAND

Typeset by Megron, Cardiff
Printed and Bound in Great Britain by
Hartnolls Limited, Bodmin, Cornwall

Cover design by CGS Studios, Cheltenham

CONTENTS

INTRODUCTION

For the benefit of readers who are not already familiar with the educational philosophy of Maria Montessori (1870–1952), it should be said that this brilliant Italian woman was one of the most influential figures in the international movement towards education reform in the first half of this century; a doctor and educationalist who for several decades devoted herself to the study of the child within modern society, from pre-birth to adulthood, and whose theories have served as a model for schools and educationalists throughout the world. A considerable number of reprints of the author's best-known books and a sizeable secondary literature attest to the continued interest in Montessori's theories and to the still lively debate surrounding her work.[1]

This book [first published in Germany in 1979] would not have been possible without the kind generosity and trust of Maria Montessori's son and heir, Dr Mario Montessori senior. He supported my idea of publishing a collection of previously unpublished texts written by Montessori during the later years of her career, and allowed me to carry out the necessary research in his private archives.[2]

These texts on educational theory and practice, which will be of interest to parents, teachers and educationalists, represent a unique selection. In addition to being previously unpublished texts from the Montessori legacy, they are also, almost without exception, unedited notes for lectures to teachers or speeches on

---

[1] See Appendix 2 for bibliography.
[2] The earliest texts in this volume were written when Montessori was in her 70s.

other occasions, which convey a vivid impression of this eminent educationalist, her eloquence and her 'mission'.[3]

This has had several consequences. In order to adhere to the spirit of the original, I decided wherever possible to include complete texts in this volume. Readers already acquainted with Montessori will therefore occasionally recognize certain passages from her books because, although she never repeated a speech or lecture and almost always spoke without notes, she always issued her audience with complete course notes, albeit in varying order and with differing illustrations and examples.

On the other hand, the directness of expression will serve to give the reader a better knowledge of Montessori's methods of work, at least as far as her lectures are concerned.[4]

Lastly however, a whole series of texts will be both in form and content completely new to the reader and will in certain circumstances reveal themselves to be of particular significance either for historical or for more immediate reasons.

This publication is therefore intended to serve one main purpose, but in three ways:

1. to show 'Maria Montessori at work', in her tireless efforts to impress upon her students, teachers and parents, as well as upon influential bodies, the importance of the child within society and within the human race;
2. precisely through the unedited form of the texts, and particularly the course notes, to present an accurate picture of Montessori and her teaching;
3. to present thoughts and approaches formulated late in Montessori's life, some previously unknown, others scarcely acknowledged, with a refreshing immediacy.

It was not easy to decide which texts to include. A certain consideration was of course given to current debate on educational policy and practice. The same is true of the need to fill in some of the gaps in the common understanding of Montessori

---

[3] The majority of these texts are based on lecture notes.

[4] For further details, see G. Schulz-Benesch, "Über Reden und Schriften Montessoris", in: P. Scheid, H. Weidlich (eds) *Beiträge zur Montessori-Pädagogik 1977*, Stuttgart 1977, pp. 139–54.

and her theories. Nevertheless I freely admit that the limited scope of this work necessarily forced me to make certain decisions over the selection of texts, which I view with some regret; because of the volume of material and of lecture notes in particular, these decisions were unavoidable.

I hope that the following texts will nevertheless be of use to parents, teachers and those with a scientific interest in Montessori's work, not only in broadening their understanding of this influential Italian – or rather cosmopolitan – educationalist, but also in pursuit of her primary objective: the promotion of an awareness of the importance of children and the problems they face in an increasingly troubled world. This volume therefore concludes with Montessori's largely unknown views on a "cosmic education".

A short introduction is provided by the editor for each Montessori text included in this volume, giving a brief summary of its content and placing it within the context of her oeuvre and of the broad spectrum of debate on education. (All notes are by the editor.)

Information on the place and time of writing is given at the beginning of each text, so that the reader may understand it from the perspective of the period in which it was written. Details of source material are appended, in the order in which the texts appear. In view of the numerous unauthorized publications of speeches by Montessori – often by friends of Montessori or by subscribers to her theories – it should perhaps be stated that these texts are all original speeches and notes written by Montessori. Occasional cuts or omissions are indicated thus (...).

A bibliography of books by, and about, Maria Montessori is included at the end of this volume, together with an index.

UNPUBLISHED SPEECHES
AND WRITINGS OF
MARIA MONTESSORI

I.

TO PARENTS

Introduction

Montessori rarely spoke so directly to parents as in the two texts "When your child knows better than you" and "Let your child keep his secret", both from about 1930.[1]

Of course she said and wrote a considerable amount about the earliest years of childhood, particularly later on in her career.[2] However, the majority of her most inspiring lectures to teachers concerned the education of children of kindergarten and school age.

The clarity of the following talks to parents is characteristic of Montessori, as is her enthusiasm, which at times is prone to exaggeration, but which she is able to contain when discussing the practical aspects of her method.[3] Her insistence that a child should be given a level of independence appropriate to his age is thus tempered by her references to the sympathetic personal relationship between teacher and child, and to the lovingly prepared physical environment of the schools.

The plea for a more human, i.e. "non-repressive" education,[4] is thus impressed upon the listener in such a way that a little of Montessori's reputed impact on her audience can be appreciated. To exemplify this

---

[1] Cf. Maria Montessori, *The Child in the Family*, Oxford, Clio Press, 1989.

[2] See Montessori's late works, *The Absorbent Mind*, Oxford, Clio Press, 1989. *The Formation of Man*, Oxford, Clio Press, 1989.

[3] Cf. G. Schulz-Benesch, 'Die Gründe der Missverständnisse der Montessori-Pädagogik in Deutschland', in: G. Schulz-Benesch (ed.) *Montessori*, Darmstadt 1970, pp. 366–91.

[4] Cf. H. Holtstiege, 'Leitvorstellungen zur repressionsarmen Erziehung in der Pädagogik M. Montessoris – ein Beitrag zur Gegenwartsdiskussion', in: *Pädagogische Rundschau*, vol. 29 (1975), pp. 267–95.

characteristic combination of enthusiasm for her beliefs and the rationality of the practised observer, an extract from an interview on "maturity theory" is appended, which Montessori gave in 1950, but which is still highly relevant today.

When Your Child Knows Better than You

I/1. ENGLAND, CIRCA 1930

If a foolish mother frog said to her little tadpoles in the pool, "Come out of the water, breath the fresh air, enjoy yourselves in the young grass, and you will all grow into strong healthy little frogs. Come along now, mother knows best!" and the little tadpoles tried to obey, it would certainly mean the end of the tadpoles.

And yet that is how so many of us are trying to bring up our children. We are anxious that they shall grow into intelligent, useful citizens, with fine characters and good manners. And so we spend our time and patience correcting them, telling them to do this, not to do that, and when they want to know, "Why Mummy?", we don't stop to find out why we interfere, but put them off with "Mother knows best".

We are in exactly the same position as the foolish frog if only we could see it. This little life that we are trying to mould needs no forcing and squeezing, no correcting or fault-finding to develop its intelligence and character. Nature looks after children in the same way as she sees that the tadpole grows into a frog, when the time is ready.

"But", I can hear you say, "shall we leave our children to do as they like? How can they know what is best for them when they have had no experience? And think what little savages they would grow up to be if we did not teach them manners . . . ".

And I would answer, "Have you ever given your children a chance even for one day of doing what they like without interference?"

Try it and you will be astonished. Watch and see how something catches their interest. Perhaps they see you turn a key in the lock and want to do it too, or help you sweep, or just make some funny little pattern with pebbles on your tidy floor, and on any ordinary day you would say, "Don't get in the way, play with your toys".

But today give them the key, try to find a little brush for them to sweep with, leave the pattern on the floor and see how absorbed they become. It is often not enough for children to do a thing once or twice, but they will perform the same simple action over and over again until they seem to have satisfied some inner urge. You will be surprised how they keep out of mischief when they are allowed to busy themselves with something that really interests them.

But if you interfere impatiently and stop some absorbing occupation, you will destroy your child's concentration and perseverance – valuable lessons he is teaching himself – he will be dissatisfied, and filled with a sense of disappointment and restlessness, and will very likely find an outlet in deliberate mischief.

And what is this troublesomeness that we are so afraid of if we do not correct little children? We say that we correct them for their own good, and a great deal of the time we honestly believe it. But it is strange how often what we feel to be their good amounts to the same thing as our own comfort. We are all so busy with our grown-up, froggy work that we forget that the little tadpoles have work of their own to do – the work of growing into men and women.

And this is work which only they can do. The greatest help we can given them is to stand by and see that they are free to develop in their own way. We can on the other hand make their work very hard. If we persist in saying "Mother knows best" and try to form their growing intellects and characters by our own standards, we shall succeed only in destroying self-discipline, we shall break the child's power of concentration by trying to fix his attention on matters which he is not yet interested in, and he will grow deceitful if we insist too harshly.

But if we change our whole attitude and say to ourselves, "Baby knows what is best for him. Let us of course watch that he comes to no harm, but instead of trying to teach him our ways let us give him freedom to live his own little life in his own way", then perhaps we shall learn something about the ways of childhood if we are observant.

CHILD, SOCIETY AND THE WORLD

This is a new way to look at the problem of responsibility which weighs so heavily on many parents. Those of us who have tried to learn the ways of childhood from children (instead of from our own ideas) have been amazed at the discoveries we have made. And there is one point on which we all agree – children live in a world of their own interests, and the work they do there must be respected, for though many childish activities may seem pointless to grown-ups nature is using them for her own ends. She is building mind and character as well as bone and muscle.

The greatest help you can give your children is freedom to go about their own work in their own way, for in this matter your child knows better than you.

Let Your Child Keep his Secret

I/2. ENGLAND, CIRCA 1930

Very few grown-ups even suspect that children have a secret of their own – in fact I have known some parents who resented the very idea that their children might want to hide anything from them.

One poor mother who always wanted to know what her little girl of five was doing every minute of the day and was continually asking questions and interfering, couldn't understand why the child had developed an uncontrollable temper, and was almost angry with me when I told her that it was nothing but the child's instinctive way of trying to keep her secret.

"Secret!" She looked at me in a puzzled way, and then added defiantly, "Joan hasn't any secrets from me. I always try to show how interested I am in everything she is doing. When she grows up I want her to feel that I am her very best friend and she can tell me everything."

It took me a long time to persuade her that if she persisted in her attitude the child would also persist in her tempers until an immovable barrier separated them. A child with less spirit might easily react in just the opposite way and become a little echo of her mother without any personality of her own, ready to share every activity, obliging, engagingly prattling, but a little nonentity. A child without a secret becomes an adult without personality.

This secret that children have is nothing so very mysterious. It is the principle of their own growth which they cannot possibly explain to anyone, although a foolish adult can try to wrest their secret from them.

Nowadays we are all so scientific, so busy trying to understand the why and wherefore of everything, that without thinking, many conscientious parents try to understand their children by questioning them. But this is asking for the child's secret, which it resents. And no good can come of such probing. When a child sees a pretty flower and wants to know its name and colour, the wise mother says that the flower is a rose and the colour is red. She has given help when it is asked and the child is satisfied. When he has absorbed that and wants to know more, he will ask of his own accord. But if the mother says to him, "Why do you want to know the name of the flower?", "Why have you suddenly become interested in colour?", the child cannot tell her. He tries and becomes confused. She is trying to probe his secret. Next time he wants to know anything he will ask his teacher[5] who doesn't ask him awkward questions back again – that is if she is one of our teachers.

When little Joan of the terrible tempers came to one of our schools for instance, she didn't know what to make of it on the first day because nobody interfered with her or asked her questions. She looked at all the material the children work with, took up the counting beads, and when the teacher had shown her what to do with them, she was left alone until she took some sandpaper letters to the teacher and asked some questions herself.

At 11 o'clock she heaved a great sigh and said, "What a lot I've done." And she had indeed tried to do a little bit of everything. The next day she did the same, going from one set of material to another but taking a little longer over each, and on the third day she became really absorbed in touching a set of figures, and

---

[5] Montessori uses the word "teacher" (maestra) as a general term for all those involved in school institutions, and therefore also – as is meant here – for nursery teachers in the "Children's House". Cf. note 37, p. 53.

there she sat for a full hour quite undisturbed, carefully tracing the angles and curves with her fingers and then writing the outline carefully on the board.

From that day she became a different child, quick at her work and with a great power of concentration – and, because no one interfered with her, we never had one show of temper at school. Of course at home she wasn't cured quite so easily, but we asked her mother to come along and see the children at work and we explained to her how important it is not to try to share a child's occupations unless it asks for help. So long as a child is actively interested in what it is doing and there is no harm in its little activity, it is definitely at work on its own development. Besides any new idea it may be grasping, it is building for itself concentration and self-discipline.

A child doesn't know why it is interested in a particular object or movement at a particular moment – the important thing is that it *is* interested, and that it is natural for its mind to grow just as its body does, therefore what interests it at the moment is appropriate for its needs.

We call our schools "Houses of Childhood",[6] and in them the children are masters of the house. When we have visitors we don't let them behave as though the children are little show objects to be questioned. Our visitors come as guests to the Children's House, and we expect them to respect our children as guests respect their hosts. Guests do not ask, "What are you doing?", "Why did you do that?", "What does this mean?"

It is useless for us to probe, for the child can no more give an account of the workings of its mind than it can account for its own bodily growth – but we can distort its development if we are not careful, we can destroy the child's sense of independence by thoughtless questioning.

Our part is to give help when we are asked. If we are careful not to interfere with childish activities and interests so long as they are not harmful, nature will see to the child's development.

Your little sons and daughters are men and women in the making. Let them keep their childish secret and you will have

---

[6] Montessori's "Casa dei bambini" ("Children's House") is for children of nursery school age (2 or 3 to 6 years old).

the satisfaction of having them turn to you for help when they need it, and you will see through the years how the secret of their childhood grows into adult firmness of character and a fine independence.

"Maturity Theory?"

I/3. EXTRACT FROM A RADIO INTERVIEW, 1950

Miss Sperry:　Dr Montessori, you said "the role of the child from its very birth". Now, how can one begin with a new-born child? I've heard a lot about the so-called "Maturity theory" – You know, "grow up first and form your ideas afterwards". But tell me, Dr Montessori, what are *your* ideas on this theory?

Dr Montessori:　Maturity has little to do with it. In fact it's my impression that the whole concept of maturity is somewhat abused in the field of education. Most psychologists seem to think nowadays that it's almost inhuman to try to teach a child anything before it's six years old. They say that learning the three "R's"[7] is a dangerous mental effort, because it's too abstract for the un-developed mind of the child, which often doesn't even understand what it's doing. This is a mistake by people who think only of the con-scious side of the mind and quite neglect its unconscious and sub-conscious aspects. My own experience has shown me that maturity has little to do with acquiring abstractions. Take language for example. There is certainly nothing more abstract or artificial than a spoken language, and yet the child is sur-rounded by spoken words from the moment of its

---

[7] Three "R's" = Reading, (W)riting, (A)rithmetic.

birth. And generally, by the time it's two and a half, the child can speak its mother-tongue grammatically. Certainly no one ever thinks about maturity or mental fatigue in connection with this marvellous phenomenon.

II.

TO TEACHERS

Introduction

The following lecture on "Children's concentration and the teacher" has been taken from the lecture notes for the International Montessori Course held in London in 1946, excerpts from which have been cited in several academic works. Montessori's theoretical lecture courses – because of her age she had for some time left the "practical" aspects to her son or to other assistants – provide a remarkable illustration of the direct development of her theories following her "discoveries" in San Lorenzo in 1907.[1] As this lecture shows, they also have an important practical content. Above all, however, they demonstrate once again that the "Montessori child" does not remain locked in a shell of isolation during periods of intense concentration;[2] instead the shell opens to expose the pearl of the child's pure intellect to its human environment. Seen only in an ancillary role, the child's teacher steps back in the "Children's House". In her "indirect techniques", her "method of love", she is a beloved, motherly figure, helping the child to grow correctly.

---

[1] Cf. in particular the first detailed description by Montessori of the phenomenon of "polarization of attention" in *Schule des Kindes*, Freiburg 1976, pp. 69ff.

[2] On the phenomenon of concentration, cf. in particular: G. Danker, "Konzentration als pädagogisches Phänomen" in: *Bildung und Erziehung* (1954), pp. 406–9; H. Helming, "Das Phänomen der Konzentration der Aufmerksamkeit in der heutigen Pädagogik" in: *Mitteilungen der Deutschen Montessori-Gesellschaft*, vol. 4 (1957); P. Oswald, " 'Polarisation der Aufmerksamkeit', das Zentralphänomen der Montessori-Pädagogik" in: *Pädagogische Rundschau*, vol. 17 (1963), pp. 1017–24.

CHILD, SOCIETY AND THE WORLD

Concentration and the Teacher

II/1. COURSE LECTURE, LONDON 1946

Concentration is a part of life. It is not the consequence of a method of education. All these deviations[3] are not illnesses, but the results of repressions. Repressions are energies which have been repressed. It is obvious that if a natural energy powerful enough to develop an individual has been repressed, the repression must be removed before energetic life can produce a cure. Repressions are not illnesses; ill people are sent to a hospital, but if we should send these difficult children to hospital, they would not be cured. Children are all wounded, psychologically speaking.

There is only one line of development which is normality. If it is disturbed in its path it becomes deviated but each individual, however deviated, has the tendency to return to the normal. If this were not so we could do nothing. So all we have to do is to set this energy free. It is as simple as that. This is not giving freedom to children in the common sense. What is the use of freedom to children, if it is freedom to develop their deviations? When we speak about freedom in education we mean freedom for the creative energy which is the urge of life towards the development of the individual. This is not a casual energy like the energy of a bomb that explodes. It has a guiding principle, a very fine, but unconscious directive, the aim of which is to develop a normal person. When we speak of free children we are thinking of this energy which must be free in order to construct these children well. We must aid this purpose. When we do, we find that the children return to this urgent energy and become normal and when this happens all deviations cease.

This phenomenon comes from the conditions of life and so the cure for difficult children must be to prepare a free life for them, and provide an environment because the environment is part of life and life cannot exist without it. This is an indirect preparation. In the right environment normality comes naturally, by itself. You must realize that you do not get very

---

[3] Montessori is referring here to a previous lecture.

naughty children transformed suddenly when they are put in the right environment. Each child has his own special form of naughtiness, each child is different and so each child reacts differently. So one day a child will concentrate on a piece of work and after this we will find that he has changed. But your eye must be trained to observe this phenomenon when it happens. We do not generally notice things like this, especially those on the spiritual side. I cannot give you spectacles to see with. When a child concentrates his character is changed. It is as though he had taken off a mask. Suppose you have a class of 30 children who are all disorderly and inattentive except two, who are normal. The teacher must be able to recognize the difference in these children. It is not so easy to see the difference because acts of destruction and disorderliness are so much more noticeable than normal behaviour. The teacher sees the defects. Again, a teacher does not interfere when a child is destroying a piece of material, because she thinks this may be a moment of concentration. People who begin to study biology must study things under a microscope, but until their eyes have been trained they cannot see anything. So the eyes of the teacher must be trained. A sensitivity must be developed in the teacher in order to recognize this ephemeral phenomenon of concentration when it occurs.

The first time I saw a child concentrate was 40 years ago. It was a child of 3 years in a class of 45 others. He was working with cylinders.[4] The others were also occupied, but the marvellous thing about this little child was the great attention with which he worked and the fact that he repeated the exercise many times. This did not seem normal to me. It *was* normal but I had studied the psychology of those days which said that little children were incapable of concentrating. When I saw this child remain concentrated for so long on one interest, I counted how many times he repeated the exercise and then I asked the teacher to get all the children to sing. They all sang and still this child remained absorbed in his work. Then the child finished just in a moment. He had done the exercise perhaps 40 times or

---

[4] Wooden cylinders of various sizes which are inserted into a block with corresponding holes.

more. He had not been disturbed by the singing. He stopped when something inside was finished, a cycle of activity. This cycle of activity finished in a moment. Something had happened inside which was of great importance even if it had only happened to one of the 45. If I had not noticed the concentration of this child, the teacher would not have done so; she would have insisted that the child joined in with all the others when it came to singing and so his concentration would have been broken.

This was the seed. You can read about it in my books. After this, whenever I saw a child concentrate on a piece of work I left him undisturbed. We must not interfere with a concentrating child, because something is happening inside that child. Gradually the other children begin to concentrate. One day one child, another day two or three children. After they have concentrated the children are different. They have no more special naughtinesses. They become detached and work for themselves. The disorderly children begin to love order. They all become so orderly that disorder is an extraordinary thing. They are exact. They enter a new path.

When the children become normal in this way, a new type of teacher is needed, a teacher who can help normality. The first thing this teacher must do is prepare an environment. She must put everything in order in the environment. She must see that the material is in perfect order. She must see that everything is attractive so that the children will like the environment as soon as they enter it. The teacher expects the children to be orderly and so she must be orderly herself. The teacher herself must be well cared for and well dressed. She must be clean and tidy and form part of the attractiveness of the environment. We must have teachers who are women who will make themselves as attractive as possible even when they are alone in the room with little children of 3–6 years. They must do something which is almost mystical and attract this little soul and be part of the attractiveness of the environment.

Mother must do this too. Mothers must not only make themselves attractive for society and for their husbands, but also for their children. When they are dressed for a great reception they must go to their children so that their children can admire them. Little children are very happy to see their mothers looking beautiful and admire them sincerely.

TO TEACHERS

The teacher must also understand that the environment belongs to the children. It is not hers because she is the teacher. It is the environment in which she helps the little child to become master of it. The thing that is lacking in society is a place for children where they are not repressed, where they have some means of development. The teacher must help the children to be independent, to keep the environment in order by themselves. She must take a great pride in seeing all these children become normalized. The teacher can be proudest of all when she is no longer necessary, because all the children are normal. She is an enormously successful teacher when she can say "The children can do everything by themselves, they didn't need me. These children are different because I have treated them in the right way. I have given freedom to these life energies, now they can go on and expand while I can retire more and more". A teacher who can say this is a great teacher, she is a teacher for life.

The phenomenon of concentration is necessary first. Then the children are calm. They move their hands only when they work. A child who concentrates does not disturb others. The teacher must recognize the first moment of concentration and must not disturb it. The whole future comes from this moment and so the teacher must be ready for non-interference when it occurs. This is very difficult because the teacher has to interfere at every moment before the children are normalized. Generally teachers interfere when a child is working. They go to see what they are doing and praise them. This praise is an interference. The teacher goes to correct mistakes; this is an interference, even though it is an interference of goodwill. It is not interference to interfere when the child is naughty but this is just when grown-ups so often say "Oh the child is so full of life", whereas when the child is working seriously they will often go and say "What are you doing? Show me". Then the concentration is broken; it is finished. So never interfere when a child is working by himself. Don't be preoccupied about whether he is making mistakes, you must not correct him at this moment. The important thing is not that the child should handle the material well, but that this material has attracted the attention of the child. The child corrects himself through repeating the exercise, or through the control of error which is exact for some of the material. If you interfere, a child's interest finishes, the enchantment of correcting himself is broken. It is as though he says "I was with myself inside. You called me and so it is finished. Now this material has no more importance for me". A child does not need praise; praise breaks the enchantment. The child is not interested in one material. It is a great inner energy, normality, which comes and you break this if you interfere.

The teacher must be very attentive and be ready to recognize the phenomenon of concentration as soon as it occurs. She must be ready not to interfere or correct. If correction is necessary she must give it indirectly at another time, never at the moment of real concentration. This is the moment of conquest, the time when the child instructs himself according to the urge of nature. Construction come through experiences in the environment and through exercises. If they are corrected at this point this process of construction is disturbed. When the children are well constructed then they can be corrected, but it is not necessary because the material contains the control of error.

The work of the teacher is to guide the children to normalization, to concentration. She is like the sheepdog who goes after the sheep when they stray, who conducts all the sheep inside. The teacher has two tasks: to lead the children to concentration and to help them in their development afterwards. The fundamental help in development, especially with little children of three years of age, is not to interfere. Interference stops activity and stops concentration. But do not apply the rule of non-interference when the children are still the prey of all their different naughtinesses. Don't let them climb on the windows, the furniture, etc. You must interfere at this stage. At this stage the teacher must be a policeman. The policeman has to defend the honest citizens from the disturbers. She must not only not interfere when a child is concentrating, she must also see that he is not disturbed. Do what you like with the rest of your class, anything you have learnt during your training or anything that your common sense dictates, it is not important because this stage is not important. Interfere by all means to stop disturbances, but we need not punish or scold or admonish when we stop bad behaviour; we can ask the child to come and pick flowers in the garden or offer it a toy or any occupation that will appeal to it. So we can amuse them today and after a time something will come from the hidden soul of the child and he will become concentrated and have a new life. He will become normalized.

We must wait patiently. It will not be long because nature urges the child to right activity. Then after this the environment must be suitable, ready for the children's development. The naughtinesses vanish and the children work in the right way.

You can do nothing when children are disorderly. If you have a whole class you cannot pay special attention to each but you can tell them all a story, you can get them to sing, you can do exercises with the whole group, e.g. move chairs without making any noise, carry a glass of water without spilling any. You can even let the children see who can do these things best because even if competition is a bad thing it does not matter at this stage; after concentration comes, competition will disappear anyway because the children will be interested in the work. So if competition is a help for practical purpose do not be afraid of using it. Nothing matters while the children are still deviated, everything will correct itself after concentration has come. We may use any means we have to attract the children's attention. Their attention is attracted through activity. Give them activity, attract them through sweetness. This also can be a method of love because we know what we are aiming at. We know that this energy exists inside the children and urges them on to do exercises which are necessary for their development. It is nature which brings the children to the point of concentration, not you. You help when you understand the idea and when you give them exercises which bring control. Give them anything which gives them an immediate interest.

The teacher must be dignified as well as attractive. The teacher must be superior and not just a friend as she is in the modern schools. The teacher and the children are not at all equals together. There are enough children in the class without the teacher becoming a child with the children. They do not need another child. They need a dignified, mature person. The children must admire the teacher for her importance. If they have no authority, they have no directive. Children need this support. If you caress or kiss them do so with dignity. The children must not be attached to the teacher but they must have

17

confidence in her. The children must be attached to the material; if they are attached to the teacher they cannot be independent. Dignity is not arrogance. To be dignified is just to be a superior person and the adult must be superior to the children because she has lived longer.

The children know that in this attractive environment they are free to choose their own occupations and that there is this attractive dignified person. An English poet wrote of a teacher that she should be like an angel, protective and sweet and dignified. The children get this sense of security when they are near this superior person. The teacher must be everything that is perfect.

Rules for the Teacher of Young Children in the "Children's House"

II/2. EXTRACT FROM A COURSE LECTURE, BARCELONA 1933

What is it that teachers[5] must do "actively" to refine their way of serving and developing human life – in the environment that has been created and adapted specially for children?

Above all, a teacher has a real duty to:

1. look after the environment in the most careful way, so that it looks clean, light and well ordered. Repair things that are worn through use: mending and repainting: or obtaining some attractive ornament. "Like a faithful servant who prepares the house for his master's return".[6]

2. teach the use of objects and show by example how one undertakes practical tasks. It must be done with gentleness and accuracy so that everything in the environment can be used by anyone who chooses to do so.

3. be "active" when putting the child in rapport with the environment, and be "passive" when this rapport is achieved.

---

[5] In the original text Montessori deliberately uses the word 'maestro' (masculine) instead of "maestra" (feminine), which she more commonly uses, perhaps to emphasize the general educational validity of these rules.

[6] Probably refers to Matthew xxiv, 45.

4. watch the children so as not to miss anyone who is struggling to find hidden objects, or anyone who needs help.
5. go wherever he is called.
6. listen and reciprocate when he is asked to do so.
7. respect those who are working without ever interrupting.
8. respect those who make mistakes without ever correcting them.
9. respect anyone who is resting and anyone who is watching the others work without disturbing him, without calling him or making him return to his own task.
10. be "tireless" in trying to offer objects to those who have rejected them; and in teaching those who still haven't learnt and who make mistakes – making the environment as alive as possible and yet keeping a concentrated silence, using soft words and a loving presence.
11. make his presence felt to those who are still looking, and hide it from those who have succeeded.
12. appear to those who have finished their work and have made every possible effort, offering them his soul in silence, like a spiritual object.

III.

ON RECURRING THEMES

Preliminary note

This section consists of four lectures, three of which were given at the previously mentioned International Course in London in 1946, the fourth at a course held at the Education Centre in Laren, Netherlands, in 1938. A few words of introduction precede each of the texts, which address some of the most frequently discussed themes in Montessori's teachings. (The first part of the section "On religious education" is taken from lectures given to nuns in London in 1937).

On Social Education

Introduction

Many authors have given a misleading impression of Montessori's views on social education, an important element in any education theory. This is especially true of interpretations based almost entirely on Montessori's writings, which fail to take into account the rest of her work and its practical applications. Montessori's ideas on social education are thus sometimes considered solely in the context of the indirect effects of what she calls a process of "normalization", which occurs as the child develops his powers of concentration.[1] Quite apart from the question of exactly what "direct" social education is supposed to mean, Montessori provides a clear answer to this kind of criticism in the following text, confirming the opinion of the renowned Dutch

---

[1] See e.g. W. Böhm, "Soziale Erziehung in der Montessori-Pädagogik", in: P. Scheid, H. Weidlich (eds) *Beiträge Zur Montessori-Pädagogik 1977*, Stuttgart 1977, pp. 109–19; particularly p. 119.

academic F.J.J. Buytendijk: "the child in the Montessori school is not isolated. He is in a microcosm of human society. The ideal reality of this society lies in unity and coherence, respect and love . . . . In their diligence in working together and helping each other, and also in their joy in play [the children] demonstrate 'we' as a reality within which each person is responsible to all others. Through their experience of social relationships they thus acquire that of true moral freedom".[2] Montessori's views on the social aspects of education are mentioned again in Chapter IV, "On the principles of the Montessori school", in which planned, tried and tested social education plays an important role.[3]

III/1. COURSE LECTURE, LONDON 1946

I have spoken about how the children learn to concentrate and how the teacher must not interfere with the child at the moment of concentration. However, the teacher must use her common sense, and at times she may interfere but not if it will break concentration . . .

It is an interesting fact that after this phenomenon of concentration the children are really "new" children. They are capable of a behaviour and an activity which is not usually seen in children. It is as though a connection has been made with an inner power or with the subconscious and this brings about the construction of the personality. We see that these children are active, that they construct themselves in a wonderful way, they create man, they are capable of work which they could not do before. These children are a surprise to everybody.

One of the marvellous things that the children showed in their work was their reaction to written language. The children

---

[2] F.J.J. Buytendijk, "Gelebte Freiheit und sittliche Freiheit im Bewusstsein des Kindes", in: *Montessori, Reihe der Forschung*, vol. 200, Darmstadt 1970, pp. 282–303; quoted here, p. 301.

[3] Cf. on the question of social education and Montessori: H. Helming, *Montessori-Pädagogik*, Freiburg 1950, ch. 20, "Erziehung zur Mitmenschlichkeit"; G. Schulz-Benesch, *Der Streit um Montessori*, Freiburg 1961, pp. 72–88; P. Oswald and G. Schulz-Benesch, *Grundgedanken der Montessori-Pädogogik*, Freiburg 1975, the chapter "Der Einzelne und die Gemeinschaft", in particular pp. 95–105.

we had, learnt to write with very little help, almost by themselves.

Many other activities come as a result of the phenomenon of concentration. One is an easy adaptation to the social environment. The school is a society. When men are together they are in a society. They are in society when they are in the home but the adaptation is different. Social life is everywhere. Otherwise there would not be a family or a country. It is the adaptation which differs. The difficulties of adaptation are not easily overcome. These children[4] adapt easily to everything, to work and to contact with others. They have a social sense like a gift. Children do not usually adapt to contact with each other so easily. So this is a new phenomenon. It is perhaps a natural thing which permits of easy communication between individuals, sympathy, co-operation, etc.

I have called this "society by cohesion" because it is not a commanded behaviour, nor imitative, because it[5] is lacking in the world as it is. It is natural, a society by cohesion. It's normal for children to be in contact with each other. It is a most fundamental fact. People who have seen this phenomenon say it is like society in embryo. It has many aspects: reciprocal help, the older children help the smaller ones and the small ones help each other. This does not mean that they embrace but they show respect for and interest in each other, e.g. when a child does something difficult for the first time, such as writing on the blackboard, another will go and admire his work. If he says to this child "Please stay and see that no one rubs it out" the second child will remain, like a soldier, in charge of the work of another so there is admiration between the children and not envy. No teacher could command the children to admire and be interested in each other's work. Everything anyone does is a beautiful thing to be admired by all, just as we admire the work of a great painter. It is not emulation but admiration, for it is spontaneous. When a child has the misfortune to break something he is very sorry, because when children have reached this

---

[4] Those who have adapted through concentration.

[5] The "free" sociability which develops under suitable conditions in people of this age.

stage, they are not destructive. They are more than sorry if they break anything, they are greatly concerned, but they handle the material so well that it is not often that anything is spoiled. If a child does break anything the others come and console him. They leave their work and help him to pick up the bits. Children can also be a moral help to each other. If one child in the class is a disturber and no one has corrected him, another child may go up to him and say something, such as "You are a little naughty, but never mind we were all naughty once and now we are good. You must become good too." The teacher could not teach things like this. She could not console a person for his badness, but to the child this badness is a misfortune and must be consoled and supported. Another thing that comes is harmony, harmony between people who work together. The material is a help, because we only have one set of material in a class, so if one child is using the piece another child wants he must wait until the first child has finished with it and put it back in its place. There is this rule that the children do not give the apparatus to each other but always put it back in its place when they have finished with it. So they have an exercise of patience and respect for others. All these little things help. They bring sympathy and understanding. It gradually brings a real harmony which could not be given artificially. Out of all this comes a marvellous order and a spontaneous discipline. The child orders his own life. This is an expression of childhood. Imagine what a wonderful thing it is. Freedom and discipline come together. This was a discovery because they are generally thought to be opposite things. Instead we find that there is no freedom without discipline. Freedom and discipline are a harmonious combination. They are strictly connected one with the other. After a time the teacher understands that if there is a lack of discipline she must be making a mistake. The children are not having sufficient freedom. So discipline controls the errors of freedom. If we give perfect freedom we get perfect discipline. Order is the basis necessary for this harmony.

The children do some things in groups, e.g. the silence lesson. The children all have the same aim and work together in order to achieve it. They all aim at perfect silence. Therefore they all remain immobile. The aim brings perfect co-operation. This is something which unites the individuals.

CHILD, SOCIETY AND THE WORLD

We can imagine an adult society organized as a constructive society on the same lines as the children's, that is on the lines of this natural society of cohesion. Attachment to other people is the first stage which brings all men to work for a common ideal. It would be good for men if society could be constructed like this but we cannot command this. It must come from nature. If nature is the basis the construction will be superior, but without this basis there can only be an artifical construction which breaks down easily.

It is interesting to see this society by cohesion of children. They have a social activity for an external purpose. Children work in a group when the active work necessitates co-operation. They co-operate when they have something to do. For example, I saw a little child who had taken out all the geometrical cards and figures and was looking at them when the music began. He wanted to put them away before joining in the music but this would have taken him some time. The other children came spontaneously to help him. This was co-operation. They co-operate in laying the table, making gardens, etc. Co-operation is the consequence of a free life with free activity.

The children then are orderly and have a harmonious discipline. A discipline in which each has his different interests. It is different from the discipline of a soldier, with his forced obedience, when all have to do the same thing at the same moment. This is a social discipline and it brings people into harmony with each other. It should be like this in the family too. The father should not order the activities of his family, but all should act harmoniously together. What is known as discipline in ordinary schools is a social error. It is the discipline of the school but not a preparation for social life because in society each one chooses his work, each must do different things but all must work in harmony.

Little by little a construction comes in these new children which is never seen in deviated[6] children. It is not usual to see a class of children working peacefully together when the teacher is out of the room. In the streets there have to be notices near schools to warn people that there is a school there because the

---

[6] Children suffering from deviancy.

children come out of school in such a disorderly fashion that they are in danger of getting run over. This is their reaction to an unnatural discipline. This other is a natural discipline with freedom as a basis.

Little by little a child accepts the idea of his group. He is proud of the world of this group. This is an expression of social sentiment. The child is happy when his group or class does well. This is a more complex kind of unity. It is a higher sentiment like the love we have for a nation or a city.

Another interesting phenomenon which comes is obedience. We think of freedom and obedience as being two contrasting things. Instead these free children are singularly obedient. Obedience must come from the formation[7] of an individual. Otherwise it is a repression. It can be the manifestation and the perfection of an individual. Only one who is master of himself can obey. If we have not this inner discipline it is difficult to obey. Children who are happy obey the teacher, the teacher who asks but who does not command. The children are proud of being able to obey. A London teacher told me how careful she had to be in what she said to the children because they were so happy to obey her. If for example she wished to tell them "Put these objects away before you go home" they would rush to obey her. So she had to be careful to say "before you go home, put these objects away".

Another question is the formation of character. A person of character is able to finish work he begins. Some people begin a dozen different things and do not finish any of them. They are incapable of making a decision. They are not sure of themselves. They need the help of another in making the simplest decisions. They are like children who cannot act independently. What can we do to develop character? If a child has no patience he cannot understand what we want if we preach it to him. If they are indecisive it is useless to tell them to decide for themselves because that is just the thing they cannot do. If you tell them they must finish a piece of work if they begin it they cannot because they get bored with it after a very short time. These

---

[7] "Formation" is used here, in a way characteristic of Montessori, to mean "construction", self-realization of the person ("formazione").

qualities can be developed only through experience and exercise. So we give these children the opportunity to practise every day of their lives. They must have the opportunities to exercise all these virtues which together form character.

These children have free choice all day long. Life is based on choice, so they learn to make their own decisions. They must decide and choose for themselves all the time and so they develop these qualities. They cannot learn through obedience to the commands of another. If they want a particular material and another child is using it, they must wait until he has finished and put it away. So they learn patience and adaptation to another's needs. It is not enough for them to have these qualities explained to them, they must practise them. Otherwise it is as though you explained a piano to a child and explained in detail how it worked and then told him to play. He will have understood all about it but he cannot play without practice. It is not enough to understand. If he is to be proficient he must spend hours and hours in practising. In the same way, how can he become an adult without learning to be an adult. If we see a man who cannot swim in danger of drowning, and if we call out exact instructions as to how to swim instead of going to help him, he will drown because although he can understand our instructions he cannot swim unless he has already learnt to through practice. Character formation cannot be taught. It comes from experience and not from explanations.

Everything needs a long preparation and much practice. So the problem of education is not a theoretical one nor is it a question of moral education. It would be easy to govern if one could make people better by sweet words. The greater part of knowledge comes through continuous practice. We may change the exercise but we must continue to study or we lose what we have gained. You may have a beautiful orderly class but if you abandon it it will be lost after a time. When children are at this stage they naturally exercise themselves. They can do much more than children of this age[8] have been thought capable of.

So I have touched on this question of the life of the class in which there is the social question, the question of character, of

---

[8] Of nursery school age.

the relationship between the teacher and the child, etc. This society by cohesion which I have talked about is a characteristic of little children, for they are naturally full of love and sympathy and help for others. They develop these qualities without help from a teacher. This marvellous activity and discipline comes naturally.

When a child is 7 years old or more another kind of social organization begins. This organization is an external one with a leader who directs it. Children in the junior schools choose a leader. We find the same thing in the Boy Scout movement. It is another kind of association. They like to have a leader to organize their activities. This is a form of association for more developed people. Little children go along harmoniously by themselves, but juniors need a leader to rule and command. They need another kind of organization, one which would have been useless for the little children who were at a different stage of development. We can compare the two forms to a piece of weaving. When a piece of cloth is to be woven the web is prepared first. All the threads lie close together but parallel to each other. This is like the society by cohesion. They are all fixed at one point but they do not intermingle. The second stage is when the shuttle attaches all the threads together. This is like the work of the leader who attaches all the people together but it is necessary to have the web,[9] the society by cohesion, as a basis or we could not weave a strong piece of cloth.

These phases are so interesting. They can form the study of the embryology of society. What are the elements which form society? The base is the individual, sympathy, love, etc. This is what the little children develop. The elements of society can be and must be developed in this age. These elements are the natural phenomenon of development. At this stage these little men are in mutual sympathy, ready to help each other without envy and proud of each other's work. If able to develop naturally in this way these children become more intelligent, interested in higher things, more capable and more attractive than would ever be possible for deviated[10] children. These children accept

---

[9] The "chain", of threads lying parallel to one another.

[10] See note 6 on p. 24.

culture, they fill every day with useful activity. They have minds which are active, hungry for something from the first moment of life. Mental starvation is a characteristic of most little children today. When they are given mental food they begin to be intelligent, they show a great power of memory, they learn many words, they absorb difficult knowledge. Little children who are normalized can do all this. It is an effect of normality.

You must see these new children in this new light. Inside man is a hidden nature and a hidden energy. The kingdom of childhood is the kingdom of heaven. If the child has the freedom to develop at this age, the result will be seen at the adult stage. It is difficult to learn cohesion at the adult stage. Little children are disciplined if they have freedom.

This is the law of the little child's world. They abolish law[11] and as in Christianity only love remains. It is essential to understand this. We must observe and study this marvellous phenomenon.

On Religious Education

Introduction

Montessori's opinions on religious education have always provoked lively debate. Although there is ample evidence, dating back to the second decade of this century, attesting to the strength of Montessori's religious faith, which is also clearly expressed in her own statements on religious education,[12] some authors suspect this to have been a particularly limited phase of Montessori's life.

The following texts, from 1937 and 1946, contradict this supposition with continual references to Montessori's earlier beliefs in favour of

---

[11] Reference to the relationship in Christianity between the Old and the New Testaments.

[12] See in particular the collection of works by Montessori on religious education, translated into German and edited by Helene Helming: M. Montessori, *Kinder, die in der Kirche leben*, Freiburg 1964; cf. M. Montessori *The Child in the Church*, London 1929; cf. summary and critical evaluation of Montessori's theories of religious education by G. Schulz-Benesch, in: *Der Streit um Montessori*, Freiburg 1961, pp. 105–58.

the religious education theories she formulated during the 1910s and 1920s; even the "parallel course" in London for nuns (accompanying the "neutral" course) illustrates the increasing importance to her of the anthropological aspects of religion, which by the time of the 1946 "neutral" course, was fully apparent: "Language and religion are the two characteristics of every group of men ... if we lack religion we lack something fundamental for the development of man" (p. 36).

Further to this theme: occasional suspicions that Montessori might in later life have turned towards theosophy, have since been proved false.[13] Some of her later statements are in fact reminiscent of Teilhard de Chardin's views. One might also attribute her recognition of the role of the church to Cardinal Roncalli, later Pope John XXIII, and to Pope Paul VI.[14] It is right that Montessori's theories on religious education, focused so sharply on the liturgy, should require thought and reappraisal like so many things in our time. But the fundamental principles outlined in the following texts still provide a firm basis, which is perhaps all the more necessary today.

Montessori's religious faith and her love for children are movingly expressed in the greeting she sent on the day before her death, 5 May 1952, to the inaugural meeting of an English Catholic Montessori association.

> Never, as at this moment, has the Christian Faith needed the earnest endeavour of those who profess it. I would ask you who are gathered together in this meeting to consider the great aid that children can give to the defence of our Faith.
>
> Children are sent to us as a rain of souls, as a wealth and a promise that can always be fulfilled; but that needs our efforts to help in bringing about that fulfilment. Do not consider the child as a weakling; for it is he who builds the human personality, and whether this personality is going to be Christian or not depends on his environment and on us who are the guides of his religious formation.

---

[13] Cf. G. Schulz-Benesch, op. cit., pp. 105–19, especially pp. 115–17; and also: R. Kramer, *Maria Montessori – A Biography,* New York 1976, p. 355.

[14] Cardinal Roncalli at the Montessori Congress in Venice, 1956; quoted in A.M. Joosten, "On Christian education", in: *Word and Worship,* vol. 3, pt. 2 (1970); Pope Paul VI, "Gli insegnamenti di Maria Montessori per il rinnovamento della pedagogia", in: *L'Osservatore Romano,* 18 Sept. 1970 (title page).

Do not consider that because the young child cannot understand in the way that we do that it is useless to make him partake in our religious life. It is among the simple people whose women take their children to church while they are still breast-fed that the staunchest faith is to be found. The child-unconscious drinks in divine powers, whilst the reasoning consciousness of the adult is but human.

It is by you who enjoy the great boon of belonging to the Catholic Faith that the responsibility for the future generations should be more intensely felt; for among you are those who have renounced the world to bring the world to God. Take then as aid in your task, in all humility and faith, the 'all-powerful children' (Benedict XV); take upon yourselves the task of seeing to it that their limpid light be not dimmed; and protect in their development those natural energies implanted in them by the guiding hand of God. May God be with you at this meeting and may He guide your conclusions and your decisions.[15]

After all that has been said it should nevertheless be emphasized in conclusion that, after 1920 at the latest, Montessori had no wish to see her teaching in any way restricted to a particular faith or creed. She wanted to live and work "For all the children of the world", for humanity and for the "Nazione Unica", to which all people and all communities would have to contribute.[16]

III/2a. LECTURE IN A CONVENT, LONDON 1937

Last time I was here, I dealt with this point: that there are certain plans to be taken into consideration in the psychological development of children. That is, different plans of intelligence give distinct characteristics to different stages of childhood. Therefore, if we are to educate the child, we ought to be careful to correspond to what we might call the psychological needs of development belonging to the various ages. Religious education also can be conceived along these lines.

---

[15] Here as quoted in Günter Schulz-Benesch, op. cit., p. 117.
[16] Cf. M. Montessori, *Peace and Education*, Bureau International d'Education, Geneva 1932, particularly ch. III/2.

ON RECURRING THEMES

I want to make it very clear that it is not that we should not give instruction to the child. Whatever instruction is considered necessary to the child must be given, but we should be guided in giving it by the psychology of the child. Therefore, I use very often a sentence which is shocking to many people, that, "we should be guided by the child". Now, when I say this, I certainly do not mean that we consider the child a responsible being who comes to us and tells us what we should do. What I mean is that far from being an empty being, the child possesses certain characteristics which may serve us as guides in instructing him.

Another thing which shocks some people, is that I say we should serve the child. These meanings are very obscure and to certain people this gives the idea that we consider the child so far superior to us in reasoning, and in other things, that we should become submitted to him and even become his servants. In fact, there is here an idea which to the non-initiated is not very clearly expressed. What we mean, is that in the child there is a divine part of creation, and that we should serve that part. We become the servants of that special part; we become the jealous guardians of that divine part, so that it does not deviate and find itself in an environment where it is difficult to keep straight. When we say that the child is guided by nature and has natural laws in him, we refer to the fact that in human nature there are certain psychological laws. For instance, when we say that the child at two years of age has already observed everything that is around him in the environment, we recognize a fact; a faculty has been given by nature to human beings, that of being able to become aware of all that surrounds them in these first two years. And if you stop to think about it, there is something marvellous in this fact.

Therefore, it is seen that the child has very strong relations with the environment which surrounds him. I call this fact, which is neither simple nor material, "love for the environment". Now, it is my belief that this urge has a very far and indirect aim. We might say, in order to understand each other better, that from birth man has a mission, and this mission reveals itself in these marvellous facts. To make our meaning clear, we say that when the child shows this love for the environment, and for what is in it, he obeys an inner urge. He being obedient to a certain inner impulse, what is left to us from an educational point of view? We must understand that this environment is not a matter of indifference to the child. Therefore, we must do something to correspond to the attraction the environment has for him. We see the small child of one or two years, who is usually given to nurses, kept in white-washed rooms with nothing around him, while we have seen that such a child is capable even of recognizing pictures and portraits.

So, as regards the religious education, we should, from the first year of age, place religious objects and pictures in the child's room. If the child sees these things around him they must have an importance. Not only is he capable of seeing things, but if you remember[17] we saw him full of love, and in need of order . . .

One thing we know: the impulses are so strong at this age, they have such power, that if one applies the religious teaching then it is as if one put it almost into nature itself. As you saw yourself from the main lectures, the child in his second year takes on impressions of the world in such a way that we recommend the nurses to take the child out, not only for the fresh air, but to take in the outside world, and if they see the child become interested in something special, they should favour him by helping his observations.

Between the ages of two and four, there is a sensory and, at the same time, intellectual stage which represents a step forward in comparison with the previous period. This sensory period must also be taken into consideration from the religious point of view. In Catholic countries, especially in olden times and among the more simple people, children of this age were taken to church. Nowadays medicine has almost forced the child to be kept at home because, they say, what is the use of bringing him to church, he would not understand anything and the church is full of microbes, so let us keep him at home. We who are defenders of the spirit of the child say that hygiene is very well and very good, but it must take a second place. We say this not only from the religious point of view but from the whole psychic

---

[17] Reference to the course.

point of view: at this age, between two and four, psychic development is more important than physical hygiene. For instance, I will give an illustration of this. We see that the child at 3 years old is learning how to eat and is taking an interest in it and when he comes to table he does not eat his hot soup. He looks to see if the fork is in the right place and if everything is there and while he is going through his observations the soup gets cold. People who are very concerned with the hygienic part say the child must be made to eat while the soup is hot and not wait. We say it is much more important that the child should be able to carry out observations which help his inner construction than for him to eat hot soup, and if we put so much emphasis on soup, so much the more should be put on religion.

So, as you see, there is in childhood a tendency which is far above that concerning material life and I should say, between parentheses, there is always this tendency towards elevation. It is natural for the mind to go towards abstractions. Also the spirit tends towards elevation and it must be understood that man does not work on a level, but going upwards. We have had occasion to observe in certain schools, how greatly the small child is interested by what happens in church. The lights, for instance, the small noises, the silence, and the way in which the people move enormously interest the children. I shall risk repeating something which I may have already told you for it serves to illustrate. In Barcelona, in a school founded by Signorina Maccheroni, a special chapel[18] had been built for children. In this chapel everything was very small for the children because this is the idea underlying our method. This chapel was meant for the children who were big enough, 4, 5, 6. In this school there were children of all ages. The big boys brought their smaller brothers. We had to have them because the families sent them. We said, let us put them in another room and they will play while the older children go to church. But we were very surprised to see the children who were so small, about

---

[18] For an accurate and detailed description see ch. 2, "The 'Atrium', or 'Children's Chapel' ", in: M. Montessori, *The Child in the Church*, 2nd ed., London, 1930; cf. Montessori's collected writings on religious education, edited by Helene Helming, *Kinder, die in der Kirche leben*, Freiburg 1964, particularly chapters A and C.

$2\frac{1}{2}$ or 3, did not want to be sent to play but wanted to come and observe, and observed with such joy that they were much more interested than the older children in what was going on in church. What the sensations were we do not know but certainly they were attracted. Therefore, we see that there is a strong sensory period in the child which will allow him to take in religion through his senses.

At this age the child has not only a great refinement of sensibility but also a capacity of understanding which is much more profound than we are aware of, and among the sensibilities that the child has at this age is the need to feel himself protected, to be sure of the feeling that he is protected. So that the religious education given by the mother at this age ought to make the child feel that there is supernatural protection; that there is a very, very powerful protection. Now the child is also very intuitive. The mother gives him at this age, as something coming from nature, the idea that there is a Guardian Angel who protects the child, and that God is interested in him and protects him, and she teaches the child some first prayers. Now, as we express it in our method, the basis is that we should give to the child what he needs for his own development and then leave him free to act for himself. In all things we must keep in front of our minds the sentence of the child who said, "Help me to help myself". Therefore we must give help in a very delicate way. We must not think that it is difficult to place in the child a religious sentiment or to give him a religious feeling. On the contrary, we must be aware that the child possesses a very great sensibility and we must be very careful and go very slowly in presenting the things to the child.

As I said, at this age there is a certain class of sensations and of feelings, and I believe a certain amount of instruction may be given by telling stories which must, of course, be chosen. First of all, the Nativity, and I mean some illustrated stories to be written for the children with many pictures, to be given with vivacity and with great simplicity. At 5 or 6 years, when he already knows how to read and write and many other things, I believe that religious instruction must also be given.

One of the things which according to me should be given the child is the story of the creation of the world. God, Creator of the world,[19] is the first logical basis of the mind. At the age of 5 or 6, I believe the child would greatly appreciate the story of order being created out of chaos. It is very fascinating and perhaps it might even be made into experiments. For instance, it is dark, and suddenly light comes. There is something soaked with water and then the water is squeezed out and on one side there is still water and on the other there is dry matter. We can show with a room filled with smoke how difficult it is to live and how necessary it is to clear the air from smoke. All this is prepared – light, separation of the water from the earth, the separation of pure air – in such a way as to make it very fascinating to the child. I have known children enormously interested in these parts. They wanted to remain a long time on the point of creation . . . they wanted to know what was in the water and we told them there were fish. They wanted to know what kind of fish . . . and the same with air, and the birds in the air. The children showed also in this instance the tendency to remain on one subject and we must give all the explanations for which they ask and answer their questions to their satisfaction, and give all this explanation on the religious side. From the age of 5 to 7, we can say that during this period we can give extensive notions to the children. We might say there are two periods of the very greatest importance to be taken into consideration; one which we might call the sensory period, and the other which we might call the instruction period.

III/2b. COURSE LECTURE, LONDON 1946

I cannot tonight give you any real help in teaching religion, that is with material, etc., but I have written books on this and you can read them. Tonight we will consider the fundamentals of religion in general.

I think that there are many wrong ideas about the teaching of religion, such as the erroneous understanding of education and the children, and the erroneous understanding of religious

---

[19] This section hints at Montessori's views on the relationship between religious and "cosmic" education; cf. introduction to ch. VI, particularly note 2, p. 93.

sentiment itself. When it comes to the teaching of religion, it is treated just like all the other subjects. Those schools which include the teaching of religion in their syllabus treat it like one subject among other subjects. This is a wrong conception. I speak against the error, because religion is something more than this. It is much greater and also quite different. It is not just a subject.

We must have a clear idea of the different periods in which it is possible to give the children one aspect or another of religious sentiment. I think that the teaching of religion must be based on the psychology of children just as I think all teaching should be.

We must remember that religion is a universal sentiment, a sentiment which is inside everybody and has been inside every person since the beginning of the world. It is not something which we must give to the child. Just as there is a tendency to develop language in every man, so there is a tendency to develop religion. Every group of men, whether highly developed or not, and at all times, have a religion. Language and religion are the two characteristics of every group of men. Religion is something which is inside every soul. You can lose your reason but you cannot lose that which is inside your heart. This is a very great question. If we lack religion we lack something fundamental to human development.

How are we to give religion to children? Well, we must not give it, we must see it develop. The sentiment is there; if it were not we could not give it and we could not help it develop. It is like a nebula,[20] a living thing which needs to develop. It must develop through the influence of the environment. We must see that the environment is right, this is very important. If we think about it, we will realize that religious education is most important at the age when children absorb most from their environment. This power of absorption is a gift from nature. At this age – up to 6 years – the child must find nourishment for his spiritual development. This essential sentiment that becomes

---

[20] Here, as in several of her later writings, Montessori uses the term "nebula" to describe the innate, as it were "pure" potential of the child's soul; she believes that for every newborn child there is a plan for the fulfilment of this potential, although the particular means of fulfilment may not yet be decided.

part of life must be taken from the environment at an age when the children have the power to take something from the environment which will remain for ever. Religious sentiment is created at this epoch and afterwards only developed. So we come to the strange conclusion that we must teach religion to very little children. I think we must teach it from birth.

We do not see religious feeling beginning from birth, but it is a fact that communities which have a strong religious feeling, are usually composed of poor simple people who take their children everywhere with them even as tiny babies. If the mother goes to church she takes the child with her. When she prays the child is there. The child sees everything that is around it and absorbs these things in the subconscious. The images go more deeply in the subconscious. At this first stage the child takes this very living part from the environment. Then, after 2 or 3 years of age, we can give something more positive, some material aid to development, because all the organs collaborate in religious development too. We cannot just give oral teaching. All the organs of movement take part and imagination especially plays a big part.

Religious teaching is not usually given to children under 7 years in schools because it is thought that they will learn enough from the mother. Others say that they will teach ethical ideas apart from religion.

I remember a lady who asked me to tell her how to give her little child an idea of God. I asked her why she thought it was such a difficult thing to do. She said that it was because the idea of God was so great. We have an idea of the greatness of God, we know God as the Creator, but surely this is a very simple thing. I believe children of 3 years can understand it. We can say "God is the Creator" to a very little child and he will understand. It is not difficult to give greatness to little children for they are great in everything. They take in all the world, so anything you have will certainly not be too much for them. Little children have a sensibility which comes from the heart. They are immersed in a spiritual atmosphere. If you speak of God among your family the child will absorb religion at home. If you say "Thank God for this or for that" it is good for the child's mind, for he has a tendency to see not only material things but to see God around everything.

CHILD, SOCIETY AND THE WORLD

It is an error to give little ideas concerning this big question. The child can take far more than he is usually given. He can take religion more easily if it is not only in the soul of the people but in the environment too.

In a religious country it is a social question. The church has feast days and days of commemoration. These are part of the life of the people. Priests, and nuns are seen in the streets. This is the religious environment and if they have this environment the children will absorb religion from it at an age when the surest sentiments must be fixed.

So take the little children to church with you. Let them accompany you to all religious exercises. Don't push the children out of the church as you would push dogs out. No place is too sacred for children. Better to let the adults go who are set and cannot change much, who repeat that they believe, that they have faith, but who are no longer sensitive. But take the children, because they have a sentiment to bring with them. They will take religion as they take language. A child can take language but if you relegate him to a nurse who looks after his physical needs only, he will not develop a rich language. It is the same with religion. If we relegate him to this nurse who gives him only material things he cannot develop a religious sentiment. So society loses religious feeling and people can come and say "Tell me how to teach my child religion because I don't know how to".

Another thing we do is to give religious instructions at a later age in the form of memorization. We treat religion as we treat history, geography or any other subject. You who have such a great idea of God that you do not know how to give it to little children, yet put it alongside everything else. You cannot have the idea yourselves if you do this, and if you have not got it, how can you give it to the children?

Children are thirsty for a great vision. They need more than a word or a phrase. I had this experience with a little child of $2\frac{1}{2}$ years old one day. It was Christmas Eve and I told the child "Tonight if you go to your parents' room, you will find that the bed is made and that they are not there. If you go to my room you will find my bed made and that I am not there. If you go to Uola's room, you will find it empty and the bed made. Then if you look out of the window you will see everything covered with white snow and you will see dark figures moving through the still night, all going to the same place. People do not sleep on this night. They all go together to church because this is the night when the child Jesus was born. The church will be full of light and all the people who go there will be full of joy. So all the houses are empty and the people are happy". This child loved the story so much, that he always asked for the story of the empty beds. If I left something out, he would always prompt me, for children remember every detail. Everything remains fixed in the absorbent mind. He remembers the great event, that the Child is born. This is the great sentiment. You cannot get this by giving little toys to the child. This is the drama, the great vision, the solemnity, the living force.

I will tell you another story about a child and his prayers. Most teachers and mothers think that it is a good thing to teach the children to pray and that when they wake in the morning their first thought should be of God. We teach him prayers like this: "Thank God for the good night and help me today and Papa, Mamma, John and Mary". The parents think that it is good for him to pray for others and so he prays for the maid and the cook, and even adds the cat and the dog. This child looked at his mother one day and said: "Let us pray for all people". It is not necessary to mention fathers, mothers, brothers and sisters; these belong to his inner soul. You think that he can do more with your help than he could by himself. You think he is a baby and give him very little things. You bring in the servants and the animals, but the child comes to realize by himself the necessity of praying for everybody.

Do not restrain the child's nature. Give him everything. Do not give small, near, material things. If we give him the idea of God and he should not be able to understand it, would it matter? It is not dangerous knowledge. So have courage and give a great deal to the children. Then they will be happy and grateful. Teach them to pray for everyone, for all the sick, and so on. Then they will have a great idea in their minds. Give religion as a revelation. If you give it as you give the rest of education you crush something from the beginning of life.

If you give children the serious things, you can give them the light and amusing things too – fairy tales, theatres, fun. We are accustomed to lies. Why worry if our joy with children comes from little things like that? Only don't confuse them with this other thing. Don't take away from the greatness in order to give futilities. The soul of the child is nourished by greatness. He is hungry for help. He looks to adults for help. Of what use is your education if you can't give it to him? Words cannot help. The whole spiritual world must be opened to him.

Special teaching is dangerous. We must not mix the teaching of morals and the giving of religion. I will give you an example I know. There was a Protestant family; the father was a clergyman, and one Sunday he preached such a beautiful sermon on fraternity: how one must love everybody especially the poor and the sick. The child understood the sermon and was very moved by it, and she left church ready to love everyone as her father had said. Children are not like us, they are more sensitive, they have a tendency to live what they feel. On the way home they met a dirty, ragged, repugnant beggar child. The little girl was so happy to put into effect what she had heard that she ran up to this child and kissed her. The mother was horrified and told her she must not touch people in the street, and asked her if she couldn't see that the child was dirty. Then the child felt that all that her father had said in church was wrong, because obviously her mother did not believe in it. Perhaps a shock like this can cancel something in the soul. We must be careful with children. Do what you like about Father Christmas, he passes away, but if you lie in real religious things you offend the child's soul. Be very, very careful to be sincere and don't play with the child in these things or with young people . . .

If truth is necessary it is necessary for the innocent, for those who have not had experiences for themselves, who rely on more mature minds. They must be given confidence because they have not had sufficient experience to know for themselves . . .

Be careful, a child's soul is like a bright mirror on which any breath can cast a shadow. Grown-up people cannot be too prudent and careful. They must be careful of the truth and careful of his great sentiment. If you have not got a vision of the child's soul, you cannot help it in its development. You must prepare yourselves first and then accept this new vision of the greatness and purity of childhood. Just as we prepared the material environment with great care, and in movement we gave the analysis[21] of movement in order to get rid of all bad movements, so now we must be still more refined when we give religion to the children. It is difficult to teach morals except in a negative sense.

One mother considered that lying was something very, very despicable ... She told her child that lying was not dignified, that it was unworthy of well-born people. She said to the child that it must be very careful and be ready to die before telling a lie. One day the child heard the mother talking on the telephone and saying "Oh, I am so sorry, I cannot come to-day. I have such a bad headache that I must go to bed". There was an awful shriek from the child, "Oh dear, my mother has told a lie".

Children are so responsive that they take what we tell them seriously. Because of this we must be very careful. Perhaps you will think that it is impossible for you to be so careful, that you are not morally good enough. What can we do? Because of the difficulty, I had the idea of preparing a special religious environment to be given apart from the other things. It would take too long to tell you about it. I have written about it in my books. In India I have given a course on religion to people of many different religions, Hindus, Moslems, Catholics, and others.

Little children between 3 and 6 years of age have a special psychology. They are full of love. They are only without love if they are ill-treated. If they are badly treated their real nature is altered. They are full of love themselves and need to be loved in order to grow. All mothers love their children in nature and so the children get this love which they need. The love of the parents is the security of this age. Their joy in life depends on the love of all the people around them for each other. The sense of security which comes from the love of their parents, is necessary too for their success in school. Children of a united family are greatly successful. So little children need to feel that the parents cannot live without them, that if they are not good their parents suffer ...

As love and protection are the necessities for this age, the religious sentiment must express love and protection, so the

---

[21] Cf. on the concept of "analysis of movement" and its practical meaning: M. Montessori, *The Discovery of the Child*, Oxford, Clio Press,1988, pp. 88ff.

idea that God loves you is exactly the right one, the one that he understands. The little child will like the idea that there are angels round to watch over him all the time, that if he is sad or unhappy, God knows. Children are full of love for us, they love this religious condition. They will do anything for us, they come to look at us first thing every morning. Think how a child admires his mother. I remember a little boy who saw a beautiful lady in a tram and who said "She was so lovely, so beautiful, she was just like my mother". His mother was not at all beautiful, but love and admiration go together.

This is the first step psychologically speaking, but if people remain at this stage they are cases of arrested development, because this is the stage of the very little child. What is sufficient to fill the soul of a child of 3 years, is not sufficient to fill the soul of an adult.

Consider the different phases in the development of the soul. At 7 years of age the child has a different psychology. He is no longer dependent on his parents' love. He wishes to be independent. He is interested in distinguishing between good and bad. So in religion we must give him a clear picture of the essentially good and of the bad things. He has an urge to have a clear distinction between the two. He has a natural tendency to perfection. The normalized child is very careful not to do anything bad. If another child is doing something which he does not think is right, he will go to the teacher and ask her if it is. The teacher may think that he is telling tales but he has really come for information – is the action good or bad? – and if the teacher tells him he is satisfied. He was asking in order to know. It is a new phase. If we look at adults we will see many who are always considering whether their actions are good or bad. There are people in religion whose job it is to purify the soul and consider every little sin. These people are at the psychological stage of children of 7–10 years. They are suffering from arrested development. Society is very concerned with morals. Morality and religion becomes a research in itself. Many people say "What more do you need?" Well, they are concerned with looking at the good and the bad, and they forget humanity. God is like a medicine to purify the soul. There must be something greater.

Then comes the adolescent. He is full of generosity. He saves humanity. Saint Theresa of Spain had this kind of development.

ON RECURRING THEMES

When Christopher Columbus discovered America and found that there were savages, she said "When you go back I will come too to help the savages." This is the third stage of development.

There are three stages of development which come one on top of the other without destroying each other, but enlarging the soul more and more. We must study these three different steps in psychology if we are to know how to help humanity.

Imagine adults as perfect. They would have no little sins. Perhaps then they could be a perfect example for children. Instead we have adults whose development is arrested at one of these three stages and the children must surpass them.

On Fantasy and Fairy Tales

Introduction

"On fantasy and fairy tales" is concerned primarily with the famous so-called "Montessori–Froebel debate" of the 1920s,[22] which has continued intermittently to the present day. Without a doubt Montessori concentrated her attention on the practical side of education; it is equally true that she occasionally spoke out too crossly and aggressively on the theme of this section.

The following lecture, which again was prepared for the course in London, explains on one hand Montessori's reasons for emphasizing certain aspects of education theory; on the other hand it indicates some of the similarities between Montessori and her eminent predecessor Froebel,[23] which have tended to remain hidden. In later life she once responded to questions about her harsh statements on the subject of this chapter, by saying that she wanted to ensure that a great discovery (that of normalization through concentration) would not be lost.[24]

I think that many readers will be interested in the opinions of the 76-year-old Montessori on this old subject of dispute.

---

[22] Cf. in particular H. Hecker and M. Muchow, *F. Fröbel und M. Montessori* (with an introduction by Ed. Spranger), Leipzig 1927.

[23] Cf. H. Röhrs, "Fröbel und Montessori, ein konstitutiver Beitrag zur Kleinkinderziehung", in: P. Scheid and H. Weidlich, *Beiträge zur Montessori-Pädagogik 1977*, Stuttgart 1977, pp. 75–85. Also: H.J. Schmutzler, *Spiel, Arbeit und Phantasie bei Fröbel und Montessori*, Dissertation, Münster 1975.

[24] Cf. G. Schulz-Benesch, *Der Streit um Montessori*, Freiburg 1961, p. 66.

CHILD, SOCIETY AND THE WORLD

The characteristic of children under 6 years of age is that it is almost impossible to teach them; children of this age cannot take from a teacher. Therefore they are considered to be too young to go to school and therefore education does not begin until 6 years of age. Another characteristic of this age is that the children know and understand a great deal. They are full of knowledge. This would seem to be a contradiction, but the truth is that these children must take knowledge by themselves from the environment.

Nature defends this age, for it is an age of mental construction and in every construction we have a law of growth. We must have a clear idea of these children. To help us understand, we can make a superficial comparison and say that these children are like chickens who peck at their food.

In a natural environment each kind of animal will only eat certain things under certain conditions. There are animals who eat certain other animals but they will not eat them if they are dead. These animals are carnivorous. They are hungry, but if they see the kind of animal which they are accustomed to eat, lying dead on the ground, they will not touch it. They will starve rather than eat it. They will eat only the living animal. They follow a definite law. Children too follow a law. They are capable of taking much knowledge from the environment but they can take it only through their own activity. They must take just what they need through their own activity. They take psychic nourishment from the environment. Their organs are enabled to function normally so they can grow and construct a normal child.

The child of 6 years can go to school. He can take part in class and get something from adults. It is as though his mind can be opened a little at this age and he can learn a little from a teacher perhaps.

We know that children since the beginning of the world take and absorb. They absorb the speech of the adults so that now, at 6 years of age, they can listen and reconstruct what is told them if it is given in a certain form. The adult gives them stories. These are the famous fairy tales. Play and fairy tales are the two things which modern observers have noted. They see play as an important instinct which brings children into the line of work and imitation of and adaptation to, the environment.

The mind of the child is open to receive from the adult at this age, in order that they may make their speech and reconstruct in their mind what they have been told. They have this power of reconstruction so vividly, that they enjoy and live in the tales they are told. They make a reconstruction in their mind, it is like an exercise. Perhaps it is necessary, an exercise like that. Through this, they can be in communication with the intelligence of men.

Children do not take everything in the same way. There must be some special characteristics in fairy tales to make them like them especially. Now everyone who knows my name says that I am against fairy tales. They say that I say they are dangerous to the child's mind. Now I have never affirmed anything that I have reasoned with my mind because if I did it would just be a theory of no importance. It would be just a matter of opinion and therefore not a serious statement. Serious statements must come from the observation of children. This is the truth. I have never before given any opinion. If I were against fairy tales, it was not because of a capricious idea but because of certain facts, facts observed many times. These facts come from the children themselves and not from my own reasoning. I have only noted this fact, that children in school[25] begin to work with their hands and are very interested in things of the external world. We noted changes in these children which surprised us. When they worked their naughtinesses disappeared without correction; timidity, capriciousness, disorder, etc., all disappeared like magic. This wonderful fact gave importance to our experiences. It proved a profound fact about children which was not known before. With these naughtinesses go other characteristics, which are considered to be very good in children, namely extreme obedience, attachment to the mother, submission, etc. These too disappear like the naughtinesses. The great love of fairy tales disappears too. For this reason I say that certain circumstances correspond in a practical way with the environment.[26] I can

---

[25] Refers primarily to the "Children's Houses" (nursery school age).

[26] Cf. on the history of the teaching of fairy tales in infancy, Ph. Ariès, *Geschichte der Kindheit*, Munich, Vienna, 2nd ed., 1976, pp. 167ff.

quote many cases in which the teacher told fairy tales to the children and they gradually went away, especially the little ones, until at last only the oldest children would be left, listening to her. The children over 6 years of age would have remained and the rest would have gone spontaneously to work. I lately had another experience in India. It was Christmas and there was a Danish lady with a fantastic mind who called all the children round her, to tell them the story of the little Jesus with fantastic enlargements. They all gathered round the Christmas tree but the little children soon went away. A few older children remained politely but as if they wished she would be quick and finish. As soon as she had, they went away quickly. So there is not a complete interest in the children's mind. They listen, or at least the older ones do, but inside they have more important urges of nature. If they are free to choose, they choose something which is more important for their development.

This has been my experience with children. For myself I like fairy tales inmensely and I like short stories. These fairy tales are very beautiful, fantastic and amusing. We like a theatre or a ball, we like to see people in strange and beautiful costumes. We are enchanted. We have this type of mind. Fairy tales are very important literature. If I could I would make a collection of all the fairy tales in the world, so that grown-ups could know them better. Some fairy tales are especially adapted to the mind of the young child, and some about princes seeking princesses, etc. to the mind of the young girl. Some fairy tales have an act such as justice as their central point. They are beautiful little stories for children, but not in place of this concentration on work. We must study what characteristics most give this treasure of concentration. We can also find out which characteristics of these tales enter into a child's mind and help the evolution of his intellect.

Fairy tales are short and have very few characters. They are very clear. The personnel are characteristic, some are all about poor children, others about animals. There is something in each tale that fixes the people or animals in an unusual way. The environment too is generally limited in the same fashion; it may be a palace, a wood, or a street, etc. The environment too is illuminated by something which touches the imagination. The imagination receives one stimulus only. This kind of material often leads to inner work to reconstruct one thing which is intelligible.

If we follow these particularities, we find that it is possible to give our ideas to children. If we use the method used by the fairy tales, we can get into communication with the mind of the child. So instead of giving just any teaching we must prepare short stories along these lines. They must have a few, clearly drawn persons with unusual characteristics. There must be a limited environment full of attractive and new things, because the children's interest is in the fantastic side, in the unusual.

Children can reconstruct every story, but they also like something that is connected with movement and a real environment. They like something they can handle so that they can fix the idea in their minds. This may be a projection of something that is inside; they construct with blocks and sand, let them construct in relation to what they have in their minds, give them something new which is in line with their natural psychology.

Children can take from the environment without a teacher. This is their natural capacity. They also have a capacity for work, which stimulates their minds. We have studied these facts before,[27] now we must see that children also have the capacity to take from stories told by an adult. We can give them stories which are like fairy tales and give knowledge under the guide of these stories. We can give history for example. The difference between history and fairy tales is that history is facts and fairy tales are invented. History is facts, but the facts are far away from us and it is fantastic. We cannot see it, we can only imagine it. History can be an exercise for imaginative construction. You cannot impart it through the senses but only through the imagination. The children must reconstruct the details.

The story of the past can be just a boring account of events. It must not be given in this way. It must be given like a fairy tale. The stories must be short, with a few well-drawn characters; the environment must be limited, unusual and very clear. They must all be built around something fantastic. History can show an environment which is very different from our own. The child

---

[27] Reference to the programme of the training course.

does not only reconstruct the tale, he also develops his intelligence, for without an intelligence we cannot understand anything. We live in a narrow environment and if we only take from this environment, our intelligence will be very poor. We must take knowledge in such a fashion that it will give us something more.

We cannot make discoveries unless we can first imagine what we are seeking. We must not think that the imagination works only through fairy tales. All the intellect works like a form of the imagination. All discoveries are the fruits of man's imagination. Imagination is the real substance of our intelligence. All theory and all progress comes from the mind's capacity to reconstruct something. When Darwin brought out his theory of evolution, he gave us an example of what imagination could do, for it was not exactly true. We cannot have progress without imagination. Many scientific theories are formed in the imagination and worked out afterwards. Theories are conceived like fairy tales in our imaginations and then reconstructed in our minds. Then the theory can be passed on to other people. In fact people can be given any theory. Many theories which are accepted by many, are later considered to be unsatisfactory and so discarded. They are received through the imagination. All have this power, those who discover and those who receive and reconstruct. So the province of fairy tales cannot be abolished in education but why should we not put everything in an attractive interesting form to be a stimulus to the imagination? We must not give knowledge coldly. If we do, it becomes boring, especially if the poor children must memorize it. All people are human beings with imaginations. Imagination is something great which reflects the light and asks for enlargement. We must give everything in a living fashion. We must not think of little children as beings who can ask only for fairy tales. They need something adapted to them, but we can give them life. The poor children who must sit in school listening to boring facts and reasons, who have to memorize them, can have only a low power of mind. These schools are mortuaries for the mind of man. These children will have dead mutilated minds.

I will not extinguish any fire, any greatness, any enthusiasm. On the contrary, I wish to illuminate the whole of instruction, so that every little particle of knowledge is taken with understanding and enthusiasm. So the mind will be developed and perfected. The power of the mind must grow with study. It must be nourished, not be bored and tired.

I have given my opinion. I believe it is the truth. I believe that a change of teaching is necessary in this sense, that knowledge must be taken in with imagination and not through memorizing. Teaching must be given so as to be adapted to this purpose. People studying must not be bored or tired; they must have greater enthusiasm and more nourishment. Schools need to have a new intellectual life. The little child cannot listen all the time. A mind that is beginning to exist cannot take in everything by listening.

We must see our new path clearly. We must give things which are adapted to our greatness,[28] which are necessary to our development. We must seek to give life to the whole of education. Then education will be a nourishment, and a means of developing a greater mind than has ever been developed before. Education in schools must help the development of man's intelligence.

Education must not be the exploitation of a poor mind, which has to memorize boring things. It is not the imitation of study which is important. We discuss how long should be spent on each study, one hour, two hours or twenty minutes. This is not a reform. The reform of education is to give life and to give knowledge in a form which is necessary to life. When this is done, the students can learn much more than they do today without fatigue. We must enlarge the syllabus. We enlarge the mind if we give abundant nourishment.

Our schools start with 45 minutes of work[29] and remain open longer and longer. The children begin to come in the afternoon. Then both the teacher and the children begin to get enthusiastic and remain a few hours longer in school. Teachers and children love it. Then the teachers begin to stay on in the evenings in order to prepare interesting things for the children next day. Are they tired? No, they are excited and stimulated.

---

[28] The greatness of the human race.

[29] Optional, or voluntary work.

Reform must be a deep psychological reform. It must not be a reform of the syllabus but a psychological reform.

The "Lesson of Silence"

Introduction

The "lesson of silence" is considered by many outsiders, and even by some people familiar with Montessori, to be more of a supplement to than an integral part of her pedagogy, and it is often treated as such by introductory courses to her work. What is more, mention of it occurs only in relatively short passages in her writings. Hearing her for once expanding at leisure on this theme, at the course in Laren in 1938, it seems to me at first glance to lack impact.

First of all can be recognized the pedagogic plea for voluntary quiet – the meaning of silence.

Then Montessori suddenly explains that she reached this way of thinking not as a result of "spiritual" or "poetic" contemplation, but as, "like everything I say, the result of an experience" (p. 53).

This experience was not empirical, but came from her perceptive observation of children; she tells at some length the story of this experience and of the origins of the "lesson of silence".

She then gives practical advice, addressing the course members directly. She mentions other experiences, develops other practical possibilities.

Finally she reflects once more: "Silence is missing from human life . . . it is therefore essential that people see this thing objectively . . . silence!" (p. 57).

Immediately afterwards she admits that when she first discovered this phenomenon she did not appreciate its intellectual significance: " . . . I was very much a doctor and psychologist, that is to say an experimental and clinical psychologist, and therefore superficial" (p. 57).

Nevertheless, as Volpicelli has said, in a fine and fitting tribute to the great educationalist: " . . . Montessori was not a theoretician[30]

---

[30] Not a theoretical systematician would be more accurate; for Montessori's work as a whole includes a significant amount of theory; the theory simply relates to Montessori's personal experience and practice, which in my opinion Volpicelli quite rightly describes.

of teaching, but an incomparable teacher. So much so that she increasingly drew the important elements from the real exercise of mastering education, to reform the positivist and naturalistic premises of her own education, in order thus to . . . acquire the basic tools of her trade by observing and being with children".[31]

This chapter thus describes how Montessori's original positivist, clinical method changed to one based on the loving observation of phenomena, followed by committed pedagogic action.[32]

The words "quiet" and "silence", as well as "composure", "concentration" and even "meditation", are used so strikingly and in such specific contexts, both in Montessori's own writings and in all the descriptive and critical secondary literature, that the "lesson of silence" can be fully understood only in the wider perspective of the meaning of silence in the Montessori method.[33]

III/4. COURSE LECTURE, LAREN/NETHERLANDS 1938

Two of the lessons in our method for young children have become very well known. I have already spoken about one, the lesson of the three times.[34] The other, which is something quite different, is the "lesson of silence"!

This is the first time that we have talked about a "lesson" of silence, and it makes more of an impression than the lesson of the three times, because everyone is convinced that a lesson has to be something spoken, that a lesson is necessarily taught in words. So how could we ever teach a lesson in *silence*?[35] Now in objective terms, i.e. from the children's point of view, this shows us something else which we want to emphasize, which is that whatever we want children to do we must *teach* them. Whereas

---

[31] L. Volpicelli, "Maria Montessori e l'idealismo", lecture (copies from Ente Opera Montessori) Rome, 27 Sept. 1957, p. 10 (private translation).

[32] Cf. G. Schulz-Benesch, "Diskussion: Montessori-Pädagogik", in: *Welt des Kindes*, vol. 2 (1977), pp. 141–5.

[33] Cf. R. Steggemann. "Die Bedeutung des Schweigens in der Pädagogik Maria Montessoris" (unpublished dissertation) Münster, 1977.

[34] On the "lesson of the three times" see among others M. Montessori, *The Discovery of the Child*. Oxford, Clio Press, 1988, pp. 251ff.

[35] In the Romance languages the literal contradiction lectio-silentium is particularly obvious (cf. in Appendix 1 the original French title).

in traditional schools, certain things which have to be taught are taught in words, while others are simply *ordered*. For example, we say "Silence!" There it is, the order. And sometimes when we ask for silence we bang on something. That's a real contradiction. It is completely illogical. Now if we want silence, we should *teach* it. And before we teach it, there's something else we must do. We must bear in mind that we have to demonstrate it and allow the children to become familiar with it. Because in general we are not used to silence; we confuse it with a certain reduction in noise, which usually leads to a reduction in disorder. However, we know that silence is of enormous value, particularly in the field of education, and that people who are trying to improve themselves or who wish to attain a high level of intellectual achievement – artists or poets, for example – need this silence. It is a necessity. So is silence really necessary? I think it is, although it is often not appreciated. When I am in a car with someone whom I do not know, and who does not know the pleasure of travelling in silence, I have to suffer because this other person thinks he has to talk all the time. Sometimes someone will say to me: "Let me sit in the back, I won't disturb you". And I say: "That's fine, as long as you don't speak to me". Now when people are visiting, it feels very strange if there is even a minute's silence; everyone feels uncomfortable and wants to remedy the situation, thinking "how can we stand the silence, the emptiness?" In Italy we say that there is an angel passing overhead! But if there is a moment's silence, when no one is speaking, we try desperately to break the silence by any means possible. And if people notice the silence, they always assume that there is no one there, because for a group of people to remain in silence, or even to try to make a silence, is unheard of. This means that society nowadays recognizes silence only as something solemn, as in the "one minute's silence". But you see, it took the Great War[36] for that to happen. It is so far away from us, yet sometimes when we are out in the country, we exclaim "Isn't the silence wonderful!" And poets too have praised silence: for example, the poet who extolled the sound – and that

---

[36] The First World War.

in itself is not silence, but rather the infinitesimal sound – of a drop of water gently falling.

Nevertheless, I have to admit that it was not this kind of spiritual or poetical contemplation which led me to introduce this strange phenomenon into the schools[37] and to teach even the youngest children this lesson of silence. For *everything I say is the result of an experience*, and experience has shown me some wonderful and surprising things. And that is why I say that *the child can teach us something*, that he can be a *guide or a light for us*. That has to be said, because children so often astonish us. What does that mean? That a particular idea had never occurred to us, that we didn't recognize it, so it is a wonderful discovery for us. This lesson has a story to go with it, which most of you may already know, or so I imagine at least. (I always assume that you know everything already, but then I suppose that if you did, you probably would not have come here.)

Anyway, I noticed that very young children of three or four – and later that even two-year-olds – *love silence to an extraordinary degree*. This is particularly surprising because we always have the impression that where there are children there is noise, that children are almost a personification of noise. That shows that even those things I say which are already accepted and proved and which could be included in a method of education, that *all these things still require a plan, based on the normalization of the child*.[38]

That is not entirely true however, because in the days when people were treating this method with some interest, when there were some people who were taking it very seriously (now it is seen by some as old-fashioned), I received a letter, saying "I am not particularly interested in this method, but I have used the lesson of silence, and it has been very useful in helping us

---

[37] Refers again in particular to the Children's Houses. Montessori uses the world "school" – as is usual in many languages – as a general term for Children's House (nursery school), primary school, secondary school; cf. note 5, p. 7.

[38] Here it becomes clear that Montessori occasionally uses the words "normalization" and "normality" (= non-deviance) in the same sense. Similarly she often uses the words "psychic" and "psychological", and others too, in the same sense.

gradually to achieve a higher level of discipline." So in that instance it was an exercise in discipline. Now it is true that you have to be still in order to have silence, but it is also true that in being silent you can achieve stillness. They are two sides of the same coin. The lesson of silence came about in this way:

In particular circumstances I asked the children not to move. The circumstances were that I was holding in my arms a little baby, about four months old, all wrapped up as babies were in those days; he was awake, but very quiet. I wanted to play a little game with the children, so I said to them "I don't suppose you can keep your legs as still as this little baby!" And I thought they would all laugh in reply. That was what I expected, because I was just making a joke, because obviously a person who is wrapped up can keep still more easily than one who is free to move. But I noticed two things: not only did the children try to keep as still as possible, they also did something that you wouldn't do, although of course you didn't see the baby; the children held their legs with their feet tightly together. This amazed me, of course, and what is more they all looked so intent and interested. So I tried to make another joke, and said "Yes, but I can think of something else you won't be able to do. Can you hear this baby breathing? You can't hear it at all – I'm sure you can't breathe so quietly!" And I thought they would have smiled at least. But, on the contrary, the older ones' faces became quite serious, and they all tried to hold their breath. And do you see, there was silence . . .

This silence was a revelation. I should never have believed that children could love this mysterious, simple thing called silence so much. Then I began to understand that there was something in this. That it wasn't the fact that I had the baby in my arms, that it was something else, a phenomenon. So I began to ask them if they had liked the silence that day, and they all said "Yes!" And then I asked if we should do it again – and they all wanted to. Perhaps they had liked the silence but hadn't understood how it had come about. Now in order to have silence, you must simply *not move*. And *in order not to move, you must think about everything that could possibly move*. So you must keep your legs and feet quite still, and your hands, and your whole body. You also have to control your breathing so that it can't be heard at all. Now this[39] will be very difficult to do, but if you want to, we can try. Perhaps you won't want to obey completely, perhaps because one of you carries on making notes, which makes a noise. In fact we have sometimes tried to make a silence, but usually someone makes notes, I can't stop them; that needs to be improved. You can hear the sound of the pencil moving across the paper.

So each of you must think about your own body, so that it is as still as possible, and that's difficult, because just when you know you mustn't move, that's when you feel you need to. When I say "Silence!" I hear all sorts of odd noises. All those noises come from someone who is trying not to make a noise, so it needs to be improved. Now I have realized that there needs to be a certain *solemnity* about this, rather than simply coming along and saying "Silence! Let's be silent! Let's all keep still!" It's something more delicate, more solemn; it really needs an *explanation* and a *preparation* of the surroundings. So I'll tell you what you must do to prepare this lesson.

The children must put everything aside, so that there is nothing on their tables. That is a necessary preparation, because the whole class must *want* to be silent, and it needs everyone's *consent* if it is to happen. So it has to be prepared. *All solemn things must be prepared!* It is worth making the effort to have the feeling that everything is in order; and this time the effort is to make everything *empty*. That is the first thing.

The second thing concerns the person himself. The children must make themselves as comfortable as possible, so that they can say "Yes, I can stay in this position." So, once they have found this comfortable position and have *stopped doing everything*, then they can try to be perfectly still, not to laugh, not to speak. And while they are doing that, I watch the children, and I say to one "You mustn't laugh", and to another "You must keep your feet quite still", etc. And as you can see, this is an excellent *lesson in co-operation*, because you cannot achieve silence in a crowd unless every individual within the crowd *wants* to achieve it for a moment. And after that the lesson is over. (Everyone does the lesson, all together.)

---

[39] Montessori is speaking about and to the audience.

You may have to begin again several times, because it requires the effort of everyone, the *agreement* of everyone, because if one person doesn't want to do it, and makes a movement, the others can't enjoy the silence any more, and then you notice a watch ticking, etc ... it is very important to understand the meaning of this lesson of silence. If you do it really well, you hear noises that don't depend on us. Sometimes there is a fly which sounds almost like a horn or a trumpet. If the silence is like that, it becomes interesting; if not, it has no interest and therefore no educational value. Then it is rather like the command made by the traditional teacher: "Silence!"

Now the results of this silence are very interesting: the children become highly *sensitive to noise*. And this is quite normal, because if you are not used to silence, you can't appreciate the different levels of noise. But now, in this silence, you become more sensitive to noise. To become more sensitive – do you know what that means? It means that noises seem *louder*, and if I do that [Signora Montessori moves the table slightly][40] you hear a noise which might have been caused by much greater force. If I tap lightly on the table, you hear a noise like the blow of a fist.

If you combine *sensitivity to noise* with *love of silence*, you will see what everyone says, that with this exercise the school becomes quieter and more disciplined. And everything you do, for example when you tell a child to put down the chair *without making a noise*, takes on a very clear meaning. Then you will see that the children take such care to put something down without making a noise, that we adults smile, because they really try to do it without making any sound at all, showing just that sensitivity to noise.

And you will understand that, as a result, if the exercise is carried out seriously, a refinement comes from that alone. For instance, to walk like everyone else walks begins to shock us with the noise; putting down objects in the normal way makes a terrible din! *You enter into a more refined, more subtle world.* And – if I may use this word – all this happens *spontaneously*, this perfection is a kind of *superior discipline*, which you could

---

[40] Observation by the transcriber.

never achieve with an order! But of course it can't happen unless you teach the lesson of silence and understand that this lesson requires the *consent* of everyone, of every individual, and that you must *teach* it, because otherwise nobody[41] would ever find it out. And also, if the exercise does not work perfectly the first time you do it, you must say to yourself, "It's because we didn't do this, I didn't pay attention to that, etc.; it's because someone moved, someone dropped something, someone moved their feet slightly, someone wasn't really comfortable." You must tell the children all that, you must make it *interesting*. But I must tell you that once I was in a school of 200 children, and the teachers had agreed to conduct an experiment to try to achieve silence among all 200 children at the same time. And the silence really was absolute, as though there were no one there; but to achieve that, all the teachers had to have practical experience, and the children had to be prepared and to have done it before. Each teacher was in communication with the children in her class, and had taught them to enjoy silence. Then you can try that experiment.

Nevertheless, silence must have a greater impact than that of simply allowing silence to be heard. It is clear that it is of far greater importance. You see, when the body is sleeping, it is at rest. But the person who is sleeping breathes too deeply for there to be silence, and the person asleep cannot hear. *Silence is missing from human life.* Silence is missing, yet all those people who are on a higher spiritual plane, all those who achieve greatness, have felt the *need for silence*. It is therefore essential that people see this thing objectively, and either demand to be alone or seek the consent of a group of people who want this: silence!

At that time, however, I was materialistic enough not to appreciate this: I was very much a doctor and psychologist, that's to say an experimental and clinical psychologist, and therefore superficial. I wanted to see to what extent the children had sharp hearing, whether any of them might be slightly deaf, how many children really had good hearing. So I wanted to carry out the usual experiments to measure their hearing. I

---

[41] The children!

resorted to the most common methods we use in our surgeries for people who are ill, and particularly for those with nervous illnesses, to test the hearing without using instruments, because they cannot bear the use of instruments; that is, to see if they can hear *voiceless speech*. Voiceless speech is generally used to test whether people are deaf: you try to speak without using the force of your voice. This voiceless speech can be heard from quite a distance, that's to say I can increase the volume of voiceless speech, yet still remain voiceless.

IV.

MONTESSORI'S "ALTERNATIVE COMPREHENSIVE SCHOOL": ON THE PRINCIPLES OF THE MONTESSORI SCHOOL

Introduction

Montessori rarely spoke from notes. For that reason the lecture which I have entitled "On the principles of the Montessori school" (India, 1942) should not be seen as a complete systematic description, but as an outline of some of the most important features of the school as explained by Montessori to the students attending her Indian course.

Current pedagogic practice, centred on the institutionalized madness of huge comprehensive schools, is dictated by predominantly external, rational, economic and bureaucratic (not to mention ideological) factors; internal pedagogic and anthropological arguments for a new education system to build a new society, go largely unheard.

In her lecture, given as long ago as 1942, Montessori presents an unbiased picture, built up from her own experiences, of a completely different comprehensive school, in which "comprehensive" indicates an anthropological rather than a short-term, school-oriented approach.[1]

The decision-making process, the development and promotion of free co-operation, and the child's attachment to one place in particular, are the key points of the lecture. Also mentioned are the "open-door

---

[1] Some earlier theories and suggestions on the form of the comprehensive school had in my opinion a similar anthropological accent: J. Speck (ed.), "Modell einer Gesamtschule", *Münsterische Beiträge zu Pädagogischen Zeitfragen*, vol. 6, Bochum 1968; P. Oswald, "Grundzüge einer Theorie der Schule", in: *Vierteljahresschrift für Wissenschaftliche Pädagogik* (1964), pp. 260–76.

principle" in a school without year classes[2], the experience of spontaneous development of a kind of "godparent role", and of the successful policy of teaching children at different stages of learning.

Of particular interest is the comparison of Montessori's initiatives with other contemporary proposals for education reform, some of which are familiar to us from her basic principles, and the reasons for her rejection of these. Such a comparison occurs nowhere else in Montessori's writings.

This entire lecture may now also be viewed in fundamental terms as a plea for the rejection of too great a state monopoly on schools, a monopoly which stands in the way of a comprehensive school such as that proposed by Montessori, and of many other valuable discoveries and initiatives.

Existing public Montessori schools, which in parts of Germany, for example, have grown out of former elementary schools, will probably be allowed to continue, but at the price of "special conditions" such as the Angebotsschule, although, or precisely because, their educational standards are acknowledged to be high. It is as if nowadays something normal can exist only in abnormal circumstances. Montessori's plea in the final text of this volume is thus particularly depressing. She nevertheless succeeds in finding a positive side even to this negative-sounding formula: after their long passage through history, people must learn about the "natural" process of the psychological and physical construction of the child, of the human race of the future, in "cultural" ways. Be that as it may, Montessori recognized and identified the dangers resulting from over-institutionalization, from the pigeon-holing of identical sets of people from nursery to old people's home, decades earlier than modern critics of our culture.[3]

---

[2] As early as 1923, Montessori had said: "Even if we had over a thousand children and a palace for a school, I would still think it advisable to keep together children with an age difference of three years. This age difference and the combination of various stages of development are one of the fundamental principles of self-education ... ". Quoted from P. Oswald, G. Schulz-Benesch (eds), *Grundgedanken der Montessori-Pädagogik*, 4th ed., Freiburg 1975, p. 98.

[3] See e.g. M. Montessori, *The Absorbent Mind*, Oxford, Clio Press, 1988; Cf. the well-known statements on this subject by Bronfenbrenner, Xochellis, Ridgway/ Lawton.

On the Principles of the Montessori School

IV/1. COURSE LECTURE, INDIA 1942

You already know what we mean by intuitive reading. It is that the child having in front of him certain objects reads the words concerning these objects, even if they are difficult (such as exist in the non-phonetic languages.) The child will also read words written in capital letters. This is not due to any magical power of the child, rather it is because we base ourselves on the plan of using the movable alphabet. This has solved the fundamental problems of dictation. I repeat that it is not a miraculous power, but that it is due to the interest that has been aroused in the child. It is the interest of the individual who has understood that there is something, a thought, attached to those signs and he wishes to penetrate into it; this interest is the fundamental urge. It stands equal in importance to the apparatus; if you were to weigh both the alphabet and the interest, the scale would be perfectly balanced.

It is this interest which the teacher must be able to inspire in the child, and then know how to educate it. This forms the psychological part of our study. If the child were not to possess intelligence, nor this vital force of interest, then you would certainly not be able to do anything with him. But I repeat that there is the natural interest in him, and therefore, you have in your hands the two forces, interest and didactic material. This interest being an individual sentiment, will vary with different children; nor will it be at the same degree of maturity in all. Now that might appear as one of the difficulties for the teacher who will ask: how am I to know what is the interest of this individual and what material is suitable to his stage of development or when would be the right time to start him on something new? You can well understand, that if (as many people think) the question rested with the teacher and her understanding she (the teacher) would find herself in an inextricable maze. For how could she cope with so many individuals at the same time?

Many of the modern methods reason that the teacher must not have more than six or seven pupils at a time if she is to give her individual attention to each one of them. This arrangement in the educational method is known as the "individual method",[4] as it recommends that there should be a few pupils in each class. Many people confuse our method with this. Indeed this "individual method" came after ours, as though an improvement upon ours and something more scientific. We however are not of the same opinion as it is not our fundamental principle to give individual education as such. There is individual education included in our environment, but it is not the teacher who gives the product of our deductions; our individual education is based on the free choice of the child.

Remember well this power of free choice. It was recognized by Decroly,[5] in the last part of his life, although he did not agree to it at first. He said that all interest could only be aroused in the child by the possibility given to him of a free choice. As you know, the Decroly method is based upon the "centres of interest"; it is a question which has been discussed a long time and much has been written on it, and the two methods, his and mine, have frequently been compared with one another. You see, Decroly places the centres of interest with the teacher, because the teacher not only seeks to have the common interest of the whole class but for the whole year as well. So this method of Decroly is one of giving instruction to others, and is therefore based on the old plan, where the teacher bases himself upon what he chooses to be the centre of interest and organizes his instruction on that.

This "individual education" is one method, the Decroly method is entirely different from that, and our method is absolutely different from both. However, we have some expressions which are common to both these methods; "individuality" and "interest". The "individual education" has mostly developed in America, and the method of the "centres of interest" of Decroly have developed in Belgium and Switzerland. There is yet a third method which appeared in England after ours. It was also derived from my work by a former pupil of

---

[4] According to Mr Montessori Sr, this refers to a method advanced during the inter-war years by a former pupil of Montessori.

[5] Ovide Decroly (1871–1932), Belgian doctor and education reformer of international renown; cf. A. Hamaïde, *Die Methode Decroly* (ed. P. Petersen), Weimar 1928.

mine,[6] called the method of "individual work". Here also there is the material and free choice, but here the free choice is not limited to the material offered by the school; there is complete freedom for the children who may even bring any material from home. The method is based on the idea that it is sufficient if the child occupies himself with some kind of material no matter what. This method has greatly spread in England; the propagator of this method also had the idea that instead of confining the children's work to tables, they were allowed to work on the ground;[7] and in such schools one might see the floors littered with all sorts of material. You can understand that in this way the child is certainly occupied the whole time, but the children do not attain a cultural development, neither is there any connection between the different activities. Therefore these schools always will remain at a pre-elementary state; for something happens like this in the nursery school. I demonstrate all these cases to give you a sort of parallel between the methods.

The trouble with the "individual work" is that the child does not find any continuity in the material he works with, and so he passes from thing to thing without there being any relation to his studies. Whereas we have seen in our method that the possibility of culture reaches further and further back to the younger child, this culture is developed upon a systematic individual work which has as its basis individual interest.

You also know the Froebel method, which is the most perfect among all the collective methods, the methods in which the teacher guides the whole class in a collective work. In the Froebel method also there is material but it is presented by the teacher to the whole class at her desk, while each child has the same material as the teacher, so that in the class there must be as many sets of material as there are children. The teacher[8]

---

[6] The name of this pupil can unfortunately no longer be traced. The fact that Montessori's statements distance themselves considerably from the suggestions made by A.S. Neill and by her pupil H. Parkhurst, is simply noted here.
[7] Montessori generally allowed this to a certain extent in some of the younger children's activities in the Children's House.
[8] Montessori generally uses the word "teacher" (maestra) without differentiating between teachers of pre-school and school age children; cf. notes to p. 7 and p. 18.

shows the material and how it is used, the children look and each child copies what he sees done by the teacher. This material is definitely established as to its quality, shape, size and colour, and certainly it is interesting. Among the different subjects to be studied in the Froebel method there are the departments of handwork, singing, and reciting simple poems. Many of these things such as the manual work, the cubes and prisms which form an essential part of the Froebel method, we also used in our first school. I shall say more, that as our method did not then exist, we used a great many of these toys. And the material of our schools today is based on the selection that the children have voluntarily made themselves from the mass of things that was placed at their disposal. This selection brought us to the conception that there must be just that amount and no more which was sufficient for cultural development. This expression which we use, "just sufficient", or "just so much as is necessary", means a certain field of material which is a selection arrived at by what was proved by the children to be their choice.

The fundamental fact in the preparation of the environment is to have only one set of each type of material. In many schools the teachers that came from our courses thought it would be better and give greater scope to have two whole sets in the school and sometimes to have three or four sets of certain parts of the material. But it became evident that the discipline of the school is hereby slackened; and if one lessens the number of sets the discipline returns.

This comparison of the different methods is a separate study which we cannot bring into our course, and which I personally have never done at any time. Our method is not a thought-out method but an experience which has come about and proved itself, and which has been given to different countries and different races, following the straight line without wavering to left or right, following faithfully in the path of the child and what he has given us. The whole of our school is based upon the manifestations given by the children, who also gave us clear indications how to organize and construct our school. In such things, for example, as the number of children there should be in a class in order to give profitable results we consider that in its best condition the class should have between thirty and forty children, but there may be even more in number. That depends on the capacity of the teacher. When there are fewer than twenty-five the standards become lower, and in a class of eight children it is difficult to obtain good results. The really profitable results come when the number grows; twenty-five is a sufficient number, and forty is the best number that has been found.

One of the things that makes our schools different from the others is the following. Most of the schools, perhaps I should say all, have children of the same age in the different classes. In fact their curriculum is based on ages. Our experience has separated us from this general rule, for in our school, what we seek is just this differences in ages. And if we were to place a limit in their difference, then we should say that there must be a difference of at least three years. Suppose you have ninety children at your disposal, all nicely classified, thirty of four years, thirty of five years, and thirty of six years. Everybody would put the four-year-olds, the five-year-olds, and the six-year-olds, in three different classes. But we preach loudly that we should *mix the ages together*, and if the room is to contain thirty children, we should not put all the ones of the same age together, but mix the children from three to six. This fact makes such a difference, that if one were to put all the children of the same age together, there would be no success, and it would be impossible to apply our method. We do not conceive of putting children of the same age all classed together. The logic of this is seen in nature; a family of three children, born at different times, naturally gives the difference in age.

Wherever our method has been developed, there was always a relation between the pre-elementary, and the elementary education. One of the secrets is the open doors. In our schools there is no such thing as a closed door which stands like a policeman barring the way. The open door to the other rooms gives a freedom of circulation, between the different grades, and this circulation is of the utmost importance for the development of culture.

One of the great advantages of our method is this living together of the three ages and it is one of the best ways for individual development. This would bring terrible disorder in ordinary schools and it would be impossible for the curriculum to proceed. Because how could there be any order? It is evident that here it is not the teacher who keeps the order, but that it is a psychological organization of the children which brings them[9] to these results. You understand how impossible it would be in the ordinary method if the doors were open, where there would be four or five teachers shouting at the top of their voices to the children, how disturbing this would be and how impossible for the children to hear what the particular teacher was trying to say. One sees the importance of keeping the door closed in the ordinary schools, for if one gave them freedom, the children who were bored would disappear, they would either go into the street or wander into the garden, and the teacher might find himself alone. When you look at the school that is organized on the old type with closed doors and compare it to the organization of our schools based on open doors, then the difference seems almost inconceivable. It requires an entirely different attitude and organization. You might ask: how do the children of one group have free communication with another group? Through the open doors. In the school in Holland the walls and doors are made of glass, and the children of one class are able to enter into the life of the other classes. The doors are quite an attraction. I remember one child who wanted to borrow the numerical rods from another room, and as he could not carry more than one at a time he went in and out several times, each time opening the door and closing it carefully after him without making a noise. And those children who were at work (not being conscious of a person going back and forth) paid no attention to it.

One of the fortunate advantages of modern architecture which received great application in our schools, was the separations between the classes made by low walls, at the level of the heads of the children. Low enough for the teacher to see in all the classes. Sometimes, in order to have a bit of colour there were curtains instead of doors. These low walls served as stands for flower vases and plants, and are extremely useful for all sorts of purposes and ornamentation. In Rome we had a school shaped like a semi-circle. It was a very spacious building, accommodating 150 children all aged between three and six years. The

---

[9] The children.

floor of this amphitheatre was divided into different apartments by these low walls, and there were no doors at all. As the room was very lofty we built a balcony all round. One had access to this balcony without needing to pass by the children. It was used for the students of the course and for visitors. In many of our schools, in Rome, and Vienna, where we had courses, the schools had such balconies for the use of students and visitors so that they did not disturb the children while they watched them at work. The only thing we recommended was that the people should be quiet. It was a very beautiful sight to see 150 children at work, and between each group a long line of plants and flowers, and aquariums with goldfish. About five elegant ladies, sometimes with an assistant, quietly circulating among the busy children; sometimes they were asked a question by a child, or they would stand watching.

What was the consequence of this freedom, where the children had not only free choice, but also free circulation? In many schools this experiment was repeated, and we discovered that each child would voluntarily attach himself to one place and would not easily move from that place. This tendency has given us much good for thought, for in spite of all the freedom it is in the nature of man to find a place where he may remain fixed. This reveals so much about the psychology of humanity, which the child shows us by his tendencies. Indeed, in this world of today where communications have become so free and un-limited, and ways of travel have become faster and faster, yet each individual will say: I want a little place I can call my own. Each man will feel this need of a place which is his home, a fixed point.

For this reason we put little cupboards with drawers in our schools. Each child has his own little drawer in which he may keep his belongings, and where he can find his possessions. This drawer attaches him to the place. It is a curious thing, this constant love of order. The children want the same things in the same place, they may move furniture and work in the garden, but they will return it to exactly the same spot. Once, I saw two children moving a table and continuing to adjust it for some time; I wondered at their action and asked what they were doing and they replied that the table had stood under the lamp and they were now trying to return it to its exact position. It is

CHILD, SOCIETY AND THE WORLD

surprising how this freedom of circulation develops in the individual the hunger for the fixed place. Now, the child who goes out of the class does not run away into the street but circulates among the other groups. This contact with other classes gives them the impression that there are things of interest going on there. This latter possibility has been of great importance in the quality of the work and the success of the schools. In Holland it became an interesting experiment, where we watched the younger children go among the older ones, and where we saw them become interested in things which we had thought previously too remote from their understanding. It was then that we realized that the young child was capable of learning much more than we had imagined. There was another thing of extreme interest. We observed that the older children would sometimes go back to the rooms of the smaller children in search of a former activity and take up the old exercises. We saw this in Holland where the school had two storeys. The older children of the upper floor would come down to the lower floor and work with the numerical rods, because evidently in their advanced exercises they lacked some clarity. This is very common; when they are confronted in the more advanced stages with some difficulty, they will go back to the earlier stages. But this never happens in the older methods of education because it would be looked upon as such a disgrace to go back! We can say then that castes are abolished in our schools; and there is not only a freedom of circulation among the groups, but also a freedom of education between the different levels and degrees of culture. It is not the class to which one belongs that is important, whether it is the first, second, or third group, but the fact that they learn from one another and thereby grow and develop. It is the idea that "I go and study where I find things which are useful to me and which I find interesting."

The main thing is that the groups should contain different ages, because it has a great influence on the cultural development of the child. This is obtained by the relations of the children among themselves. You cannot imagine how well a young child learns from an older child; how patient the older child is with the difficulties of the younger. It almost seems as if the younger child is material for the older child to work upon. I have often stopped to watch them and thought; is it not a waste of time for the older child? But then it became clear to me that when you teach something the subject becomes clearer for you. There is nothing which makes you learn more than teaching someone else, specially when you don't know the subject very well. Because the struggles of the other act like a control of error for yourself and urge you to acquire more knowledge in order to give him what he needs.

In our schools it was clearly visible which child was the special pupil of the older child who taught him. This possibility in the work of our school is of such importance that the development of the classes would be of a much lower standard if there were not this contribution. Then we went on experimenting, and brought older children of twelve and fourteen into the classes of the younger ones and asked them to instruct the small ones. It was so interesting to see how much more rapidly they learnt in this way. It made us think that there is a gradation of mental development, and that the difference between the adult and the child is so great that the adult cannot give the same help to the small child as can be given by one who is nearer in age to that child. That is why it is said that one must be as a child to understand a child. It is a great help to the teacher to have these different ages in the school; and you must understand that to have success you must have these different ages.

These are the things you should remember: primarily the *interest of the child*, which brings the child to fix himself on the study. Secondly, *the co-operation of the children,* and this is immensely aided by the fact that the ages of the children are not alike; the older children are interested in the younger, and the younger in the older. So we come to the conclusion that not only the older ones can help the younger ones but they will also profit from the fact. Thirdly there are the *human instincts which bring man to attach himself to one place, and which result in order and discipline.* It is curious that the remark mostly made by visitors is that their strongest impression is of the silence that reigns over the school. The most fervent activities of these children are carried out in a silence that had never been imposed on them.

This will give you an idea of the fundamental organization of a school along our lines.

V.

CHILD AND SOCIETY

Introduction

Just as Montessori's theory of "normalization" is sometimes described in terms of a "productive utopia"[1], this same notion has also been used to explain her opinions and suggestions on the subject of "the child and society". The question is whether the term "productive utopia" is intended to be an essential feature of education theory. In the lecture on "Children, teachers and society" we hear Montessori answering questions posed by members of her audience at the 1946 lecture course in London; by piecing together these replies and explorations – given in Montessori's inimitable manner – it is possible to arrive at a whole new concept: the identification of social conditions as a reason for the development of faults in children and as a means of correcting or avoiding them.

If this lecture reveals the anthropological and – according to modern understanding of political parties – almost apolitical basis to Montessori's thought processes, one might be inclined to believe that the same would be true of a politically neutral statement such as that made in Madras in 1940 on the necessary "protection of children against exploitation". Certainly she denounces the political exploitation of children in "totalitarian states" and gives ironic but forceful warnings, which are still valid today, about "committee" decisions on what is best for the child: ". . . the state knows how to treat the child better . . ." she says, warning against simply changing the agency of exploitation. But the question remains of whether a kind of "Ministry for the Child" such as she suggests, could guarantee in the long term

---

[1] W. Böhm at a one-day conference of a German Montessori Society in Frankfurt, 8 Oct. 1977.

the measures for protection and support which she feels to be necessary (p. 82).

Montessori's views are made even clearer in the section I have called "Work as an anthropological necessity". Here she puts to one side current problems of social tensions in favour of thoughts on the subject of a "new epoch", the "one nation"; one choice: peace or ruin.[2] Without the possibility of true peace – which forms a background to all her later writings – all her own and all other initiatives towards educational reform, far from building a "productive utopia", become mere charades acted out on the brink of disaster. She pins all her hopes on true humanity in which work is more than a means to an end: "man works just as he breathes, and because it is a form of life" (p. 84).

Nevertheless, Montessori's analyses of the reality of education, such as those she gave in the lecture "On the schooling of young people" (in Rome at the age of 80), are still particularly stimulating, not least because they demonstrate the small steps which everyone can take towards participating in this hoped-for future for the human race; in part they are highly relevant, for example when Montessori states: "All the reforms in education to date have therefore been made on a false premise; and they are cruel because they only make study more and more empty. They ignore the fact that one doesn't have to lighten the load, one only needs enthusiasm." (p. 89).[3] Traditional secondary schools create "... tiredness, confusion, inferiority complexes, anxieties. And then we talk of democracy!" (p. 92).

---

[2] Logically Montessori speaks at another point about the *final* revolution through education: "Society has erected walls and barriers. We must tear them down to reveal the open horizon. The new education is a revolution, but a non-violent one. It is *the* non-violent revolution. After that, provided it succeeds, violent revolution will no longer be possible." (6th Indian Montessori course, 1944, Lecture 22; cf. *The Absorbent Mind*, Oxford, Clio Press, 1988. Cf. M. Montessori, *Peace and Education*, Bureau International d'Education, Geneva 1932); also: *The Unconscious in History*, Madras 1949; cf. G. Schulz-Benesch, "Einige Hinweise zur Frage der geschichtlichen Einschätzung Montessoris", in: *Montessori-Werkbrief, Folge 33/34*, Aachen 1973, pp. 46–9.

[3] Montessori argues not for a reduction in formal education but for an educational, psychological reform, which would avoid the negative consequences of the anthropological burden of failure; cf. *From Childhood to Adolescence*, 2nd ed., New York, Schocken, 1976; interest and achievement correspond in Montessori's view in the same way as freedom and discipline, which she describes as "two sides of the same coin" (*The Absorbent Mind*, op. cit., p. 260).

CHILD, SOCIETY AND THE WORLD

To conclude the introduction to this section it should be mentioned that texts V/2 and V/3 are based on the notes made by an Indian listener, which in places are hard to follow. However, I did not feel authorized to make more than minor alterations to these; see also general introduction.

Children, Teachers and Society

V/1a. COURSE LECTURE, LONDON 1946

You have sent me many questions which you would like to have answered, so that now I have a long list. You have asked me to speak on moral education, social education, normalization, the intervention of the teacher, and the relationships between the parents, the children and the school.

These are all old questions, questions from the past, it is as if an ancestor had come back to ask them. They come from the prejudices of the common idea of education. Moral education is spoken about in the special sense of correcting moral defects. Education without this is not understood. Moral teaching is the basis of the old education. How many times have I had it said to me "Take the stick away from the schools and we teachers can give up"? Correction and teaching is the basis. It has been thought that we must teach morals and set a good example. The parents and teachers have co-operated to train, punish and be an example to the children. But just look around the world to see the people, and then imagine that these people must be the moral example for the future citizens of the world.

Another question that is frequently asked is, that if children develop individually in our method, how can they be prepared for social life? This would lead one to suppose that society is composed of individuals who are not developed. But why should these two things be in opposition? Society is composed, so how will the composition of society be affected if the individual is helped? If the children develop individually they do not live as hermits. The children do not develop as hermits or become solitary hermits, isolated in a mountain cave. Morals are the rules of society. They do not exist without society. Good and bad is what can be done to society. Otherwise there would be no morals. If you shut one deaf and one dumb person up together in a room, what moral education could you give them? Could you tell them not to crush the fly, or what? It is evident that morals come from a social relationship with other people. So it is absurd to imagine education and a moral education without society. We have a wrong basis for education. It is wrong to think that one person has to give everything, morals, character, etc. It is an error to think that these things are separate, because all together they form a unity. The human individual cannot develop without a social life. When you ask me how to help the development of character I can only say that I cannot develop character. What can I do in order to give people character? This is an old-fashioned idea. But all these questions lead to much more serious questions.

You cannot have a programme for moral education because moral education must be different at different ages. Children are not the same at all ages. Up to age 6 moral education must be according to the psychology of this period. There are many errors in the children's behaviour which people will correct. This special moral behaviour in little children is called "naughtiness". This naughtiness is not a real moral question. Today we do not call these children "bad", we call them "difficult". There is a modern problem, the problem of difficult children, and it is an almost insoluble one. The goodwill of the parents and teachers does not touch the naughtiness of these difficult children. So another set of people has arisen in answer to this practical difficulty in modern society. There are the doctors of psychology. These psychologists have founded special institutions called child guidance clinics for these difficult children. The new idea is "guidance" not "imposition". The clinics are rather like hospitals. So this is the great development of modern society: difficult children are put in hospitals instead of in a corner of the schoolroom. These incorrigible naughtinesses are like illnesses. The parents and teacher can do nothing and neither can the doctor, for the difficult children become more and more numerous. In the old days the question was not so important because the children were subdued by punishments, but today it is like a flood. It is as if the Thames or some other beautiful river should overflow. That would be a disaster. The number of naughty incorrigible children increases in our world today and the adults begin to be helpless. Everybody is trying to find the cause of this badness in children.

We must not think that in 1946 the children are suddenly worse. It is not a result of evolution, children must be nearly the same as they have always been. So it is not the children's fault. It is not a question that is only attached to the children. Conditions for children today are supposed to be the best there have ever been. They are well fed, have good clothes, plenty of fresh air, gardens, parks, schools, parents that are more understanding about liberty and freedom. The poor parents are disillusioned, disappointed. This question must be different from the common questions of the correction of children, the setting of a moral example and of giving good physical conditions.

The cause must lie in the lack of some element which is essential for life. We must try to find this element which is lacking. This is the research that is needed today to help everybody. This missing element must be something psychological, something psychological which is either not known or is not taken into consideration . . .

It must be that there is something lacking in the treatment of children everywhere and of every age. We must take a new element into consideration. Perhaps man's behaviour has changed in this complicated world, perhaps he disregards something fundamental and family life is different and the children are the first victims of this disregard. We must consider children from this point of view. Moral and social education are so closely related that we must have some new contribution for moral hygiene. It is evident that these children suffer. It is evident too that modern psychology is not sufficient. All the things we have had up to date for moral education have not been enough. The facts prove it. The question of moral education is not as simple as it was before. Some other element must be added to correlate with the present form of society which is different from what it was formerly. Moral and mental hygiene especially must be developed in order to protect children. The relationship between the family, the teacher and the children must be harmonious because the school environment plays a larger part than it did before. Both the teacher and the parents must have the help of psychic knowledge that was not known before . . .

Goodwill alone is not enough. Today we need a positive contribution towards the betterment of the human soul. There must be a mental and moral hygiene towards which family, school and city all make a contribution. This will be the progress of civilization.

The progress and the growth of the individual are very important. Progress is the care of the psyche of the individual in relationship to the environment. It is not a question of doing something for the individual first and then something for society, for it is in society that the root lies. We must see the individual in his place in society because no individual can develop without the influence of society . . .

When I see how the numbers of naughty and difficult children are increasing today, I see it is not a question of the morality of the children, of something wrong inside individual children. It is a question of a lack in the parents more than in the children and attention should be directed to them rather than to the little children. If we are to make better conditions for the children we must consider the parents.

There are three things. First change these grown-up people who are so anxious to give little children a moral education. Grown-ups must adapt themselves to the needs of the times. The central point for little children is their need to go in a certain direction towards the adult. Adults are ignorant and see the children in only one aspect. They see only the naughtiness of the children. So the conclusion is that if we are to have a better humanity the grown-ups must be better. They must be less proud, think less of themselves, be less dictatorial. The adults must look at themselves and say "Yes, I understand this problem."

V/1b. CONTINUATION OF LONDON LECTURE V/1a

We came to the conclusion yesterday that the question of moral education is a very difficult one, and one which is not as simple as it had generally been considered. That it does not consist merely in correction and preaching nor is it possible to deal with it through direct teaching. It is a big question correlated with psychic life and society as a whole. We must consider all the factors which lead up to moral education.

One of the contributions of our experience is to know that we must not consider the teacher and the child as two people, the teacher as one who gives the principles of morality and punishes the child. Education is something direct and complete. If we have a teacher who teaches morals well, it does not follow that the children of that class will become good, moral men. It is not so simple as all that. There is another side: the environment and the mode of life. The teaching of morality is indirect. The adult, the child and the environment are a trinity. They have to be considered as one thing. The principle that the environment is of fundamental importance was first given by us, but many people now understand this principle. The environment, especially within the limits of the school, is of fundamental importance. The environment is important for man too. Another conception that we have brought to life, is the importance of the child's psychic development. I have told you how children do not get their abilities through heredity, but that they possess potentialities through which development can come. This development comes through a precise order and through some well-determined laws of growth. Every individual has an inner urge. You remember how I told you that the urge in the unconscious began. Something powerful is there which is the creator of the child's personality. This creation is marvellous because it comes from almost nothing. First there is only the potentiality, and the child, by taking what he needs from the environment, grows to be what he is. Nature gives some help. We have already considered this ordered power of nature in creating the human child. It is a very delicate and wonderful thing which must be cared for. It is like a psychic embryo. All the organs of the body develop in the physical embryo so delicately that nature defends it, but the psychic embryo does not have this strong defence. Nature gives some help, e.g. maternal love. But this delicate construction comes into an environment which is not prepared for it today. It meets with many obstacles. If the physical embryo had to meet with such obstacles it would result in a monster. Each child would have a different physical deformity. As the psychic embryo encounters obstacles in the environment we get many deviations from the creative natural line of development. These differences in right development come from the beginning of life, especially from 0 to 3 years.

It is because of this that children of 3 years of age in our school are not just the sweet angels they should be at this age. The nurses say they are devils and the mothers only want to give them to the nurses to look after; the teachers wonder what they can do with them. They all say that the children are impossible, that they are capricious, bad-tempered, destructive, inattentive, etc. Grown-ups say "I can live with cats or dogs, but don't give me children. They are too much for me." I have heard many people say: "No sacrifice is greater than to teach little children and nothing is more difficult." Why is this so? Because the monster is there, not the child. We have a quantity of little monsters under our care. What can we do about this most difficult practical problem? When these horrid children are older and can adapt themselves to the adults' commands, the teacher in the Junior Schools will be able to manage them with a stick or punishments. Many mothers agree that the teachers must punish their children. The parents punish them at home and so they sympathize with the teachers. Then later as a result we get boys and girls with criminal tendencies. We get many juvenile delinquents. This happens because the inferior morality and behaviour[4] to us, not because of any fault of theirs, but because we think they come into the world bad and full of naughtiness.

If the children's behaviour depended on their parents, teachers might be able to choose the kind of children they would like to teach. They might say: "I will only have the children of sweet mothers in my class" or "I prefer the children whose parents are strict because these children behave better." Instead teachers know that children are all the same whatever the parents are like, that sweet mothers may have capricious children, and so on.

What are repressions and what causes them? It is not only I who say this from my experience, the whole world now realizes

---

[4] The inferior moral code and defective relationship with the environment into which they were born.

that repressions come when the forces of growth, that are the creative forces of the psychic personality, are repressed. Children are repressed when they cannot have the special activity that nature imposes on the human personality in order that it should grow well. All the disordered psychic movements of children come from two sources in the beginning. The first is mental starvation. This seems strange to us because we have always thought in the past of the child's mind, as being empty and passive. We did not know that it needed nourishment, that little children could have mental starvation. The second thing is lack of activity. If the children are left in an ignorant state, expected to be passive and sleep a great deal, naughtiness must result. These are repressions. The children cannot develop because all acquisitions come through experiences in the environment. The children are capable and have a marvellous ability to absorb from the environment. If they are isolated from the world, put in a prison, without stimuli, they will lack something fundamental. If they are made to sit still and are forbidden to move and to touch, their natural activity is repressed.

Bodily illnesses can come not only from the construction of an organ, but also from its wrong functioning. So bad behaviour, what we call naughtiness, is wrong functioning. It is an expression of deviated development, not normal development. Our experience has taught us that the bad behaviour cannot be corrected by direct means. Neither can sweetness or good treatment directly stop it. We have found by experience that the only way to be successful is to put these children in an environment which will not stop their creative activity. We must give them another chance, another form of life. We must not attempt to correct their deviations, but we must give them a more normal life in which their bodies and minds can be active, and an environment which will contain many motives of activity. We must give the children freedom and relaxation from the continuous direction of adults. So we give them the right environment, relaxation and freedom from orders. This is an indirect treatment; it is not the correction of the individual but the preparation for a new life. This is something children have never had, even in the grandest and richest of homes. For even in a palace, you find that the children are relegated to some obscure nursery.

CHILD AND SOCIETY

The new man came into the world and the world would not accept him. There is no place for him to lay his head.[5] We must prepare an environment in which the child can live, this will lead to the good child.

The psychologists who run the child guidance clinics know that the family is not enough today. They say that these difficult children should be taken away for a time from their families, where they are too rigidly treated. They must be given freedom from adult people, servants, teachers, parents, nurses. It is like a breath of fresh country air after city life, it is like a country holiday. These psychologists say the children should go away for varying lengths of time according to the individual. Poverty is not responsible for these difficult children, for many of the worst come from rich homes. In the beginning, the environment to which these children were sent contained many possibilities for activity and there was a spy-hole in the door through which the grown-ups could watch the results, whereas the children did not know they were being looked at. The children were left free to have a holiday surrounded with toys. They were left alone. But they remained ill, just as a criminal remains ill after a time in a prison and is always having to be sent back into prison, so the children came back to the clinic again and again and are not cured. Perhaps this is because the environment given has been a material one and is not enough. Perhaps they must be free of the repressions of the parents but not from the parents and not from society. We must not isolate these difficult children but give them a place in which they can live freely and in which they are not detached from their mothers and fathers and the rest of humanity. There should be a place where they can spend some hours each day doing what they wish to do and where there is no tension. Many such environments have been prepared and we will speak of these in the future. The children do not become little angels immediately. They behave wrongly but they have a teacher who looks at them with love and hope and who is ready to help them in their invasion of a new world.

---

[5] Refers again to Christ in the New Testament (see John i, 11; Matthew viii, 20 and Luke ix, 58). Montessori's sometimes bold theological images and comparisons have occasionally been criticized.

CHILD, SOCIETY AND THE WORLD

If you have given children freedom and a good environment
and they are still disorderly, then you must pray to God to help
you, because then these hurt children cannot be helped without
a miracle. All we can do then is to wait for the grace of God. Do
all you can and then wait for the grace of God. This is the central
point of our schools. This is the point from which everything
comes. One day one child may concentrate. Another day
another child. Little by little you get the phenomenon of real
concentration and once this happens everything good comes
from this concentration in interesting work, in which all their
faculties are concentrated. This phenomenon comes through
interesting work with the hands.[6] The children work with
exactness, with attention, they repeat the same exercise many
times. From this concentration comes the real change in
children. I don't know exactly what happens in the psychic life,
there is some realization of the plan of nature. It becomes
possible for all the functions to come together, there is some
contact with the different parts. It is like the creation of a new
personality. The children's naughtinesses disappear. It is like a
fairy tale, only it is true. It is a miracle. Functions which could
not function before because they were repressed, can now
function. We get the unification of all the energies and the
creation of a new person. We call this normalization. This
phenomenon of normalization only comes through intensive
activity and real concentration. People doubt this ability for
concentration in little children because we are different from
them and we cannot concentrate our scattered energies. After
this concentration comes, you see the child as he was meant to
be; before he was not. It is as though you had a child whose
features were all mixed up, whose eyes were in the middle of the
cheek, whose hands were where the feet should be, and then all
these parts become ordered in the place nature meant them to
be.

After this new child has come, education is possible. You
could not educate the child as he was before. Now he is
readjusted, you can educate him because he is in a condition in

---

[6] For the significance of the hand in the process of becoming a person, compare
Montessori's comments in: *The Absorbent Mind*, op. cit., pp. 136ff.

which he can develop and in which he has much to develop. The path of education is a long path. There are many exercises which will be useful and many things which can be taken from the environment. We can give all the good things and all the high things and the child can take them. He could not take them before, and because he could not, people thought he was incapable of taking them. Now he is in a condition to take them. This is the joy of education, the education of the mind and of the practical life. After children are normalized they can take the whole of education. Therefore the great hope for education is to help the little young humanity which is in our hands.

Protection against Exploitation of Children

V/2. EXTRACT FROM A LECTURE, UNIVERSITY OF MADRAS 1940

We may take up again two points which are of great interest, one of them is the great value of childhood from the social point of view, and of this there is no doubt. But in the recognition of the value of the child, there is the danger of this value being exploited for aims which are useful to adults and not to the child. And I would like to explain this terrible mechanism of humanity which is obsessed by this disease; if it finds anything of value, instead of making use of it for progress, it tries to grasp it for itself, an attitude which is dangerous, and especially so for those who cannot defend themselves, such as children. So, we should always remember this forgotten citizen and when we wish to do something for him which represents social progress, we must always take precautions to prevent adults from taking advantage of this value. So, it would be necessary to have two sets of laws, one set which promotes progress in the child, and the other set which defends the child. Otherwise it would happen as it does in totalitarian countries, for instance, that the child's value is seen to be in a certain direction and that he is exploited for national aims. Or, as happens in other countries, the child is not taken into consideration at all and there is no progress and the child is completely abandoned. So, it becomes really very, very difficult to give a child freedom. It is a complex social question, but the solution of this problem is, above all, in the hands of the teachers themselves. But it is also in the hands of the fathers, and although among the fathers there are those who defend the people, they do not know how to defend their own children. So the question of the child citizen is the most important question of the day. For instance, during the short period in which there was the socialist regime in Austria,[7] the child was greatly valued and uplifted to a high level and very many beautiful institutions were made for children. But immediately everything went wrong, because the state said, "All these children are ill-treated by the family, the state knows how to treat the child better." So, they took the child away from the family and immediately the exploitation of childhood began in one form or another, with one excuse or another being made. As you see, the defence of the citizen is lacking and the defence of the citizen can come only from adults who see things clearly, because the children cannot organize everything by themselves. So it is not a question of preparing a law about children, it is a question of awakening the public consciousness to two facts: one is that the child needs a world of its own, and second, that the child (the forgotten citizen) needs to be defended from exploitation. So we say that the fate of children must not be given into the hands of a committee of people who decide what is best for the child and that is the end of the matter. This committee must discuss the problems from different points of view and when they have discussed and have come to a decision, those decisions are made to become laws and once it has become law, we might say we are almost there. If you look at the laws, especially those made for children, you will find, when you take into consideration the legal part, that there are no laws for them except that the child's act might as well be the adult's act as far as citizenship is concerned. The consciousness of the value of the child is lacking and this consciousness is absolutely necessary for the progress of society. That is why I have been preaching for the last several years that there ought to be a body or an institution for the protection of children, something like a "Ministry for Children".

---

[7] Pars pro toto: this clearly refers to Vienna, where between 1918 and 1938 the Montessori method had a strong influence, at least in a specific ("psycho-analytical") interpretation.

On the other hand, adults make many efforts to obtain certain rights for their citizenship, for instance. You have certain parties and trade unions and you have speakers and representatives of Parliament as well as newspapers and magazines and all these intelligent people do just one tiny part of speaking about one small right of man. And tell me where there is to be found a meeting for the cause of the freedom of children, for the freedom of the only being who is incapable of defending himself and incapable of speaking for his own rights. There is not even the slightest thought of its needs. And those who work so much for their rights and for the rights of the other oppressed people and so forth, who are they but fathers of children? It would be advantageous to have the fathers start along the path of social practice to defend the rights of children, because they would understand the social problems better. Once I was at a meeting of nothing less than the Communists in London and they had the holy patience of listening to my speech with the translation sentence by sentence. I drew a parallel between the communist ideal such as they preached it and the conditions of the children. And I was telling them, "You want these things for yourselves, but how do you treat and how do you consider your children? If these are really the sentiments that you have about human rights, why is it not in your power to start applying these principles for your children?" So, you see, there is something which is entirely lacking in the conscience of humanity. There is an empty space, an empty spot in the consciousness of society and what we ought to do is at least to make society realize and feel this . . .

Work as an Anthropological Necessity

V/3. CONTINUATION OF MADRAS LECTURE V/2

When I started, I said there were two points on which I wanted to speak again. What I have said just now is one of them.

Now as to the other point: the question of work. People have this orientation that they work in order to find a means of livelihood and it is certainly true. One must live and the means of livelihood are given by work – that is certain. It is also true that we must have feet in order to walk but it is not true that because we ought to have feet in order to walk, that all our body is composed of feet alone. That we must work in order to live is true, but that is not the whole story nor is it the aim of work. If we work with this aim which is not the real aim, then everything comes up wrong side out. The school also treats the child from the same point of view: that school is there to give to the pupils the notions which will make them find a living; that it has only that purpose of securing a means of livelihood. And so the wrong plan of education comes up and this plan has been constant until now. We must study according to that law and we must study in order to pass examinations; we must push and urge the children in order to arrive at the point of passing the examinations. And this routine lasts not for one day, but for the whole of school life, and by doing this we learn what we might call a "manual art of the brain". All of us, no matter if we are doctors, teachers or professors, we all take the thing as a job, just as much of a job as the fishermen who go to fish. It is a means by which one man makes his own living. And if there are differences in human beings and different classes, there is one thing which is common to all of them – each seeks the kind of work which brings him money. And it is only just that one should work and find a means of living. But the child is conscious of another kind of work which has its origin in life itself. If it were true that man need not work in order to live or man did not work in order to find a means of having enough money to get food and clothing for himself and his family, that man would work just the same, because man works just as he breathes and because it is a form of life. Without work, man would not be able to live without becoming ill, degenerate and old, and that is why work is one of the essentials of existence, of life. Men are urged to work by a need which is higher than the instinct of self-preservation, and a man who no longer works for himself or for his family is a man who does the great work of the world.

There are a great many examples of men who work without any need for money in order to live and then work becomes something grand, a fact which makes us think somewhat about the child who walks and walks without ever getting tired, and who works and works because that is the need of its life. By working in this fashion, he arrives at an inner level and he does not think about examinations and of what class he is in. He does not think about what kind of work he is going to do in life, whether he is going to be an engineer or a teacher or whatever. We have thus been able to put together children of different degrees and levels of culture, because what interests them is the work itself and they do not feel any artificial pride and say, "I am in the first class, he is in the second and you are in the third", and so on. This class distinction of culture does not exist and what interests them is the work and they are all together working. In the centre that we started in Holland, we took into consideration the syllabuses of the ordinary schools, and put on the noticeboard the different items of culture that were needed for the 2nd, 3rd and 4th classes, saying that children who know this lesson and the other belonged to this class or the other. We saw these children go and read this list with great interest just as if they were citizens who went to street corners where notices had been put up. One of the children, perhaps a 7-year-old child, who ought to be in the first class looks at these lists and says with great indifference, "I will be in the third class." And it is a matter of complete indifference but they go back to work – and this is what is of importance. If the work comes from an inner source, it is much more intense and much more fruitful. There is greater progress and one is led to think that perhaps even in society the work of man could be better if it was based upon natural laws. That does not mean that one forgets the needs of life or that one must work without making any money, but that one feels a great passion for work and one works beyond what is necessary. It is the understanding and love of any work to which one has dedicated one's life. The vision towards which the aim of work leads is so strong that one gets all one's energy from work itself. This is a fact. Then fatigue disappears, sloth disappears, and man multiplies his energies in an extraordinary way. There are very few examples of these because when work is squashed, as it is today, there can be very little comprehension in society. But work as it is now, is like the work of children in ordinary schools; people work as if they were slaves. They work for an exterior aim while work ought instead to be the greatest expansion of the human soul. The few examples that are available reveal what adult man is capable of when there is something which drives him, when it is the inner motor instead of external necessity that leads him. Now, of these motors there may be many kinds. There are some that are weak, some that are strong, just as there are real motors of 2 horse power, 8 h.p. or even 100 h.p. What is of importance is not the motor itself but the horse power which is inside, and also that they are driven by their own motors. Work might be governed by the organization of all these motors, but when adult man is also grasped by this urge of work, he does external things . . .

But, even if one has to work for money, nevertheless one may do so compelled by a great urge and a great interest.

In conclusion, I want to say that all work, even of the most modest kind, can be done because one feels an interest in it, that is, work for work's sake. So it is necessary that work should be based upon this vital fact, that man in order to exist needs to work. And also in the work that we do, we need not work with the aim of becoming a headmaster, or a supervisor or an inspector of schools or to make more money for ourselves or for the family, but because we have something in view before us, because we have understood the value of the child, and because we have to work in the better interests of humanity.

Now I shall say a last word. If the states were independent and everyone made enough to live and enough for all their lives, and if one had no economic independence just to the extent of having enough to live, then one could give all the strength to that which is the urge of one's own soul. So that economic independence is not the fact to which all the human energies should be attached as a final aim. It should be the contrary: all the human energies might go forth along the path to which the interest of soul leads . . .

I have no time to say more, but you must see this: that one of the greatest urges of humanity which keeps society going from progress to progress is this irresistible inner urge for work, and it is one of the laws and one of the facts that childhood has revealed to us. We see it stated in our religion that we are in this world in order to *love, know* and *serve* God. Work is one of the methods and must be based upon these three laws. The work of humanity that always loves more, knows more and serves more, that penetrates more and more into details in order to become more and more interested, can be translated in the three words above – love, know and serve. This is the basis upon which human work ought to be founded.

On the Schooling of Young People

V/4. COURSE LECTURE, ROME 1951

In education one must assist life, especially in the crisis periods of growing up: one of the most complex and critical periods is that of adolescence.

Adolescence depends on vital factors such as physical phenomena, and in education one must take special notice of these phases as they affect the body and as the child passes through them.

The child is a being who has special physical characteristics which change with growth and which determine distinct phases that greatly affect his future. Education which does not take this into account is badly mistaken.

This question is neither pedagogic nor biological, but it is a social matter because all men form part of society, even babies, and even young people from 10 to 20 years old. The men who make up this society have clearcut characters. For example, we live in democracies, but for this to be really true, everyone must be democratic or rather, everyone must live in a democratic way, even those who come between the ages of 0 and 20.

But it is a good idea to keep in mind that from birth to 20 years, these men are not democratic or at least are not so during their formative period. The formation of a man evolves in a way that is anything but democratic. What happens to a life in adolescence? There are no choices. Study in a certain school is compulsory, and certain work must be done whether it is pleasant or not. The work is done without using the hands and the children must stay, I won't say sitting on chairs, but "embedded in their benches". They are crucified to a piece of wood and there are nails there too – they are the eyes of the teacher who is feared and who makes fright gush out of the child's and the adolescent's soul from the very start.

It would be something if they were crucified for an ideal! But these adolescents have been condemned to a sacrifice for no purpose! They must stay there without moving, listening (without working) to a monotonous little homily, lessons that are like pieces of a mosaic containing history or geography, given to them by the teacher's droning voice.

Can these children escape from this? No. At this point one has to ask why one section of humanity is allowed to express its free choice for a government that it wants by voting, while the other half cannot show its own will in the same way. How can the soul be formed in such constriction? Children have no choice either in their school or in their teacher, nothing. Education understood like this is no education for the man who wants to grow into something great. There is no provision for such an approach in education today. In schools nobody takes the slightest notice of the treasure that lies inside an individual, or of his dignity, or of the possibility of actively "becoming someone" in a collective sense. In normal education these attributes are not recognized. In school, the adolescent is destined to listen for an hour to the teacher who speaks on a prearranged subject. After the hour is up, that teacher goes out and another comes in to talk about something completely different which has no logical connection with the preceding topic, and so it goes on. The young person has just begun to absorb one set of ideas when he is asked to jump to another. What can he do? Nothing, he must just listen, motionless, nailed down, crucified on a bench that tortures him and all the others![8] . . .

The new education has had an influence all over Europe. In order to relieve the suffering, teaching programmes have been shortened, parts of grammar, geometry, etc., having been removed from each one. But have the young people benefited from this? No. They can be compared to prisoners who have been jailed for life, who must work, but to make life easier for them their working hours have been reduced. They will be helped only in the sense that they are working less, but they will always remain prisoners. But it should not be a question of relieving pain, mental fatigue, boredom, dislike – and our reform has

---

[8] This powerful image is also a reference by Montessori to her earlier criticism of schools in 1909; cf. *The Discovery of the Child*, op. cit., pp. 12ff.

nothing to do with this. It is based instead on a hitherto undiscovered passion which comes from the children's own desire to study without force or direction. So, it is not a matter of relieving a heavy weight, but of presenting study in a different way. To work properly, this reform must operate according to the needs of each individual intelligence. The brain always asks for work which becomes more complex. A child with intelligence will have the desire to climb higher and to better things. If a man's fundamental needs are satisfied, he changes, and his character changes too.

So, the labour involved in learning becomes easier, not by studying less but by enriching the studies themselves. We have seen that children do not have minds that grow in little pieces like mosaics in which they can fit pieces of geography here, and pieces of history or biology there. Their mental and spiritual needs must be satisfied as clearly as possible. All the reforms in education to date have therefore been made on a false premise; and they are cruel because they only make study more and more empty. They ignore the fact that one doesn't have to lighten the load, one only needs enthusiasm . . .

One cannot stay at the same level all the time. We have to go forward, we cannot stay still – it's like riding a bicycle. We must go up or down. At the moment, humanity is on the way down.

Even though the human race is going through one of the greatest periods of scientific discovery, ploughs the oceans, rushes across the earth and flies, it has so many strange and incomprehensible illnesses to deal with.

It is said that so much is done to save democracy. But how can we save that if we don't save the quality of life first? If the point of human life is lost without trace and without fruit, it is a poor lookout for our children. At school and at home, they are always led, always told what to do, always forced to work. Their fathers say: "Poor boy, he's always there, studying from morning to night, he's a real slave to his books!" There can be progress when the relatives understand. Think about it, parents, is it right that they should go through the same process that you experienced? It is a social duty to understand the function of growing up and the state of education in schools.

In Roman times, those who were set free from slavery were not called free men but "freed slaves". Someone who has once been a slave can never really be free in his innermost being. That is what happens to those of us who are full of frustrated ambitions. This is the conscious part of oneself, but there is also a subconscious part which can never be brought back to life.

There is a new form of education which works from the belief that it can free young people from misery at school by giving them a lighter curriculum. But this clearly does not work in the children's best interests. This is proved by the increasing number of juvenile delinquents, of whom only a few are children who have been abandoned. Nowadays the authorities' only solution is to pander to this state of affairs. But instead of looking for remedies, would it not be better to realize first that delinquency comes hand-in-hand with adolescence, and to prepare for it, as villages once did? For such things are not confined to one particular village, they occur all over the world – it is a universal condition. In the past people have tried to conquer what has already happened. Nobody seems to have had the idea that prevention is better than cure . . .

Nowadays everyone worries about babies who have been abandoned or who are ill. But there are many children who are much worse off and who go completely unnoticed. Today one helps the unfortunate, the sick, delinquents: they are our "brothers". Love your brother. It seems a very unbalanced state of affairs. But this is happening in our time. But we are aware of a part of the human race that does not attract our attention or sympathy. We call it a privilege to study: those who go to school are lucky and those who do not are not. All parents have this ambition for their children. But their situation is really very sad. And it still has not dawned on the collective imagination because if it had, it would be acknowledged. Society takes care of those who are abnormal, but not of those who are called normal. But are they really so normal? We are a race that does not feel any satisfaction in itself but only heaviness, labour and boredom. And this is a direct result of having been to school.

The condition is determined by the school which has no means of relieving it, or of raising humanity to a higher level – and such a school often makes it worse. Every child who goes there falls prey to that state of mind known as an "inferiority complex". Not only does he not have any freedom of action, he is tormented by the lack of it. He is made to notice his weaknesses all the time, not because the teacher actually tells him he is stupid, for that would be an insult they could respond to. Nobody blames you then if you answer back. But these children cannot escape the feeling that they are intellectually inadequate. And the more this happens, the greater the inferiority complex – "if you don't do these exercises well, if you don't study these lessons properly, I won't put you in for the exam". It's impossible to answer such an argument. It is not a threat, it is a consequence. If I threaten someone in everyday life, he can defend himself by threatening me back, but in this case it is impossible – one thinks, "I want to but I can't, I'm not sure of myself, and if I don't pass the exam, I can't be sure of my future. What will my father say? What about my friends?" This state of mind grows more and more pervasive and causes insecurity. Insecurity alone is responsible for delinquency. "I haven't a family to be proud of, I haven't got a future, I'm not sure what my life will be, I feel driven by misery".

And the others are insecure too because the teachers do not want to help, understand or comfort them. Instead their attitude seems to reinforce the underlying feeling of failure. What grows in the soul as a result of such continuous treatment? First insecurity and then fear. If I could save myself from this bad woman, from this wicked man . . .

Fear starts when we can't convince ourselves of its cause. We educate children to feel afraid when they are growing up. They are afraid of everything: of their fathers who despise them, of the teacher who can fail them in their exams, of the principal who is not the slightest bit interested in their feelings and who does nothing to help them. "He wants to help me but he can't because I'm inferior". Who encourages him? Who helps him? There is nothing else for him but fear. Fear! Minos![9] Hell.

So first the insult and then fear. This is the way they are subjugated. "Who will save me from this state of mind?" Certainly not the father who is hardly going to say "You failed because you are a misunderstood genius", but instead ". . . I told you that you would fail!"

---

[9] In the Italian text the word used here is "Minosse", i.e. Minos, the ruler of the underworld! Cf. the linguistic connection in Italian: inferiorità (inferiority) and inferno (hell).

Thus all the preparations for life are based on fear. When pupils at the Montessori schools in Paris and in Holland (which are not perfect) go to take their exams, they make a great impression on the state adjudicators. The latter often ask where these children have studied, because, oddly, they show no fear.

In our state schools, we cultivate fear, and this is not an insignificant factor but a real danger. For if someone has a tired mind, he has an inferiority complex, he is afraid of the superior human being, he is afraid of not knowing how to respond. My fear is that in such a case the mind cannot remain open to new ideas, it cannot give out, or mature, and this will lead to strange cases of children who have studied a great deal but who even so cannot respond, and cannot learn any more. These are spirits which cannot be resisted. The people who come out of such schools are almost beaten, they are powerless to resist temptation, they have no great ideal. They come out tired, confused, full of inferiority complexes and fear.

And then one talks of democracy! It is more apt to say "We liberate that part of humanity from a state of tyranny and slavery". It is good to understand them and to help them to get on. One of the most important things is to give these adolescents a conscience again and to find a way of rehabilitating them as is the case for delinquents or the sick.

This is the grand design from which greatness and beauty can be created. It is one of the most burning of all social issues.

VI.

MAN'S PLACE IN THE COSMOS

Introduction

In earlier 'histories of pedagogy", even in some still in use today, the value of Montessori's work is acknowledged only for the practical methods she devised, with at best an emphasis on her deep almost reverential "love for children".

But even in Montessori's early writings there are astonishing passages which might have drawn attention, if only by implication, to a broader basis to her thoughts and methods: "In education we are now concerned not so much with science as with the interests of the human race and culture, which has only one nation – the world" (1909).[1] And in her thoughts on religious education an early reference can be found to the "study of creation" (1929), which goes far beyond the "object-oriented" side of universal education.[2]

This concept of universality, which is at the root of all her ideas, was clearly apparent by the time of her speech on peace in Geneva (a speech which received scant publicity in Germany). It was her belief that, despite all his discoveries and achievements, man is sleeping at the edge of a precipice: he must turn his gaze away from nature, which he has successfully dominated, and look into his own soul, which has been

---

[1] M. Montessori, *The Discovery of the Child*, Oxford, Clio Press, 1988, p. 5. Interestingly, Montessori added the words "not so much with science as. . ." only in a later edition of the text.

[2] M. Montessori, *The Child in the Church*, London 1930, pp. 23ff; cf. concerning " 'Cosmic education' in Montessori's education theory", the important essay of the same title by P. Oswald in: P. Scheid and H. Weidlich, *Beiträge zur Montessori-Pädagogik 1977*, Stuttgart 1977, pp. 122–38.

neglected.[3] A new humanity is the goal – which Montessori believes must be achieved through the child, since life is more readily understood in its developing form than in its adult state. Responsibility lies with every individual, not with one particular group: "The whole of mankind is one and only one, one race, one class and one society." "La Nazione Unica"![4]

"Man's place in creation" is an exceptional one, the full weight of which people do not comprehend; an integral part of creation, and yet different in potential and in reality: "In simple words – if God moves beings intelligently, to man He gives intelligence itself" (1935) (p. 98). As they watch over future generations, people must never forget this if they are to be saved.

In the (much criticized) certainty of her belief in her mission, Montessori has gone far beyond the stage of party politics: she has entered a new era, which has already begun, and behind which are lagging individual states and parties, which are vying for a role in the future of mankind. This is why, in her notes on "Communism and peace", she says: "peace cannot arise from a purely economic formula" (p. 101). She nevertheless reproaches an imperfect democracy for its faults, in her notes on "Teachers and the realization of the democratic ideal", and even rejects a direct link between education and an "ideal [which is] hard to define" (p. 101).

But what does she think should be done? In answer to this question she firstly describes her "cosmic theory", which explains the origins, context and responsibilities for man of "life on earth". People do not fully obey the laws of creation, and thus risk becoming the victim of the "supra-nature" they themselves have created. She believes that this, together with what we now call environmental problems, is a far greater problem, affecting the whole of mankind.

People are still "so unconscious" of the fact that they have become united, "that the evidence of this union has presented itself to them more in the form of a threat of destruction than in the guise of a superb triumph of creation" (p. 109).

Montessori believes that a "universal consciousness" (ibid.) must be awakened and cultivated within children between the ages of six and

---

[3] M. Montessori, *Peace and Education*, Bureau International d'Education, Geneva 1932.

[4] First Indian Montessori Course, lecture of 14 Nov. 1939 (A).

twelve, since they are particularly receptive to this idea. After explaining in detail that "in this union every man is dependent on other men and each must contribute to the existence of all", she calls for the awakening of a feeling of "gratitude and love" towards all people, and for the condemnation of offence to human life, if we are not to incur the "curse of God", which will "visit us again and again in the shape of disastrous wars" (p. 113).

This final lecture, certainly the least known and possibly the most unexpected text in this volume, is still highly relevant today in its moving appeal for obedience of the laws of creation, in a way which could scarcely have been imagined when it was written in 1945.[5]

Man's Place in Creation

VI/1. LECTURE IN A CONVENT, LONDON 1935

Here are some ideas, some directions, to emphasize the modern points in our theory. (Modern criteria generally make a psychological study of the child; for instance, what has been said of guiding instincts).

Let us give an illustration of one of the marvels of nature. We have always considered these as a manifestation of the divine. Creation has been admired for the beauty of its effects. We have admired the butterfly for its beautiful colours and the birds for their plumage. These are taken as manifestations of the divine. Meditations have been made on these subjects; even children have been taught to meditate on these things. But all this is but admiration of objects of sense.

But here we have another factor – not visible but immaterial. This is the Spirit, the Divine Spirit, intelligence, acting,

---

[5] Contemporary tendencies, such as peace studies, environmental studies and educational initiatives concerning the relationship of highly developed industrial states to the "Third World", appeared in an embryonic form in Montessori's "cosmic education".

It is worth mentioning here that in the last years of her life Montessori also made an intensive study of the specific details of an appropriate teaching method, and she published several short works on this subject in India. "Cosmic education" has for a long time been a compulsory theme of the training courses of the Association Montessori Internationale.

guiding. The tiniest creatures have their guide which leads them on step by step. It is as if we came to understand the secrets of creation better from these little things than from bigger ones. First we see things in construction and then things constructed.

If we think of the child as being guided and constructed, we are spectators of the work of the building up of man. What was said of the Breathing of the Spirit is illustrated here. The great value which these manifestations have is the respect which we feel for them and with which we must look upon them. The modern studies of biology are all on these lines, e.g., the instincts which are much more striking than the observance of exterior things. All this shows the intelligent operation of beings. It is an intelligence which urges them to operate. One example is that of the butterfly resorting to a plant with which it has had nothing to do and laying its eggs on the underside of the leaf. It does this because if the eggs were on the top they would be washed away by the rain. The butterfly does not act with intelligence, but in an intelligent way.

Another example is the spider. Far removed from the beautiful things of nature, it is a dark creature with the disagreeable instinct of spinning webs to catch its prey. When the spider must attend to her eggs she forgets her enemies and makes a thick web, a kind of sack with double walls so that the air can pass between the lining and the outer wall. Thus all inside is kept warm and protected against the damp. Man has taken a much longer time to make the same discovery. It is a mode of getting one's bearings in the world which the spider has known from the beginning of its existence.

There is one type of work in the world which is not very attractive to nature: that of the scavenger insect. This insect has to clear away certain substances which encumber the earth. We should take a broom, but the insect rolls the substance up into balls which are bigger than itself. These balls are perfect spheres. To do this would be a problem to us, but the sphere is certainly the geometrical body which is easiest to roll, so the insect carries out its own special work. This is one of the marvels of nature, this harmony which preserves the world. Everyone has an active mission, so that every being has this merit – that it works and tires itself. It is not that God has created the world, but that every creature has an inner activity the merit of which is contemplated by the scientists of today.

So we must think of the child having his own directives. In the child's development we see a *logical* directive. Soon after birth he is sensitive to the *order* of things about him, then he begins to observe the striking things. In his second year he begins to observe tiny things which we do not notice at all. He also begins to act for order as best he can and this is logical for in this way he has a basis in his inner self from which he can act. He is getting ready to act in the world. The child follows out a logical guide and like a traveller in an unknown country he must take his bearings and study his surroundings. Then he will notice minute details. All this is done with great enthusiasm. In this way he follows out the common laws because of the guide within him. Other beings learn to do things but always the same things; they roll their balls and spin their webs and so on, but always in the same way in obedience to their instinct. What distinguishes man is that he has *no* limits and can adapt himself to anything. It is strange that although man is the being with the greatest possibilities he is the one who remains the longest inert. Lambs can follow their mother after birth, stand on their own feet and soon reach a state in which they can live with others of their kind. Man needs one year before he can walk. This is because the muscles of man are not directed just by instinct as are those of other creatures. The individual himself must animate his motor powers. Each one must prepare himself for his own individuality. It is in this diversity of individuality that we see the difference between man and other beings. This animation of the child's own muscles has for us a great importance. It gives as it were *the secret of life* which will accompany us throughout the development of the child. We have given to it a name which perhaps does not quite define it: incarnation. Every psychic urge is like a tempest blast which awakens the muscles (e.g., speech); it is as if the psychic guides of the child created his activities, so that as he grows he must always be active.

For instance, the tiger cub will move according to its instincts as will also a young deer; but man must act for himself as the motor organ in man is inert and it is he who must give it activity. Then it is that the child must be left free to act. When acting during the first year of his life, the child is creating himself not by intelligence because he is not yet able to understand, but by instinct or psychic urges. These inner guides enable him to reach the intelligent stage. He constructs his intelligence according to his inner guide. He becomes a conscious individual whose intelligence is similar to that which we see working in nature so that the human individual does not incarnate an instinct but a soul. Then the individual possesses an intelligence so that if everything is guided so also must the intelligence be.

In simple words – if God moves beings intelligently, to man He gives intelligence itself. If there is a divine communication between all created beings here there is a more direct one. (Human instinct can communicate with the divine. It is as if man alone understood that he must take this line.) This has been found in human remains since the beginning (stone remains and idols). Among the most striking discoveries about primitive man are these remains of religion. Man has always prayed, and has always sought a guide by prayer. All this would lead to a conclusion in education – that we must take into consideration that from birth the child has a power in him. We must not just see the child, but God in him. We must respect the laws of creation in him. We must not think we can make him; if we do, we are spoiling the Divine work. If we consider it is we who are forming the child we are not constructing the active part in the child. We are diminishing the powers of the human creature. If we consider that it is we who are to construct the child we are really materialists. What does it mean to be materialistic? What did Science say when accused of it? When Science said that everything came of itself and God had nothing to do with it! What are we but materialists if we act so? A strange thing happened in (scientific) materialism: observation showed bodies (not only of men) as a kind of laboratory of organic chemistry, and it was thought that certain things could be put together to make a man. It was said that the secret lay in chemical mysteries which would give the necessary results, and then we should create a man – 'homunculus' – something small and stumpy. This was to be the great triumph of the School of Materialism!

In Education we are acquainted with the psychic reaction of the child. The child is for us a psychic laboratory where we find the elements from which a man can be built up. If we put together the God-given elements we think we could make something greater. We think it is we who can create a spiritual man. But in education we are always disillusioned. The results are always small, stunted and deformed. Then we worry ourselves to solve problems which have no solution in this way. If we are to solve these problems we must no longer be materialists.

The secret of education is to recognize and observe the divine in man; that is to know, love and serve the divine in man. To help and co-operate from the position of the creature not of the Creator. We have to further the divine work but not substitute ourselves for it, otherwise we become seducers of nature.

What we are apt to say is "Obey me and be like me." What we ought to say is "Obey God and become like God." We think we say it because in words we are constantly telling the child to obey God but our actions do not agree with our words.

There are two things to do: give a knowledge of God and all the things of religion; and recognize, admire and serve the inner forces of the child and humbly set ourselves aside with the intention of co-operating so that the personality of the child with its inner presence is always before us. This must be the basis of education. The task set before themselves by masters has generally been to mould soft material and fill empty vessels, but we must set ourselves to see the marvels hidden in the child and help him to unfold them.

Communism and Peace

VI/2. NOTES, LATE 1930s

If communism were to conquer the whole world and all men and women had security of life and equal rights, even then peace would not come. This is because the human individual holds latent psychic energies that, as yet, defy control. Also a fundamental part of knowledge is lacking: the science of the psychic construction of man. An illustration in the physical field will this clear.

Before medicine became a science, great epidemics were treated somewhat similarly to the way the great social cataclysms are treated today, attributing them to supposed personal influences. Therefore the real causes could never be removed. The individual diseases were treated following certain prejudices concerning the external manifestation of the patient, a method which made it impossible to discover the real causes of the ailments.

Medicine became science only when it was based upon knowledge of anatomy and physiology, that is upon functions and organs that do not appear externally and when, with the aid of the microscope, it was possible to discover germs hitherto invisible.

The social needs of men as considered by Communism are only external manifestations whereas the actions of men may depend upon psychic constructions.

Where do men and women come from? How have they formed? Through the Child.

This places the question of humanity upon a universal basis, namely nature; and not upon a social detail, as happens if we consider the question from the point of view of the workers and of their economic conditions of life, in a society which as yet has not completely evolved.

Everyone, men and women, to whatever class they may belong has been built up from the child, and if the child is ignored all humans come from an unknown origin.

Did they grow in good conditions or not? We cannot know without knowing psychic embryology, that is the psychic development of the child during the first unconscious period, during which the child builds the *psychic box* as mysteriously as he forms the physical body before birth. In order to carry out such a study of the psyche it is necessary to go beyond mere exterior observation and the intelligence of the scientist must act to penetrate the psychic secrets, as if he possessed a microscope for his mental sight.

Are men developed to the maximum of their energies or do they possess repressed energies? If their activities have been artificially repressed, do we not go back to the old point from which revolutions begin: oppressed man? Certainly some other unexpected revolution must result from it.

Does what men would enjoy in a worldwide communist regime represent all the welfare that man needs? Does man live only for his present? Does he have needs, or better and more powerful hidden urges which lead him towards a future which is different and superior to the present?

If it is so, men will inexorably create new prejudices and new idols.

Is the intelligence of man, as he is today, developed to the maximum point? Or does the average intellectual acquisition of the masses leave aside a powerful intellectual urge, such as the one that in evolution has led human society toward an unceasing progress? In this case the merely utilitarian culture will leave a void which will gradually fill with ignorance: ignorance which will urge man to seek and demand new rights. Then, old causes of rebellion will raise their heads anew.

There will again be agitators, revolutionaries, idolators, ignorant perturbators.

Communism does not bring world peace: peace cannot arise from a merely economic formula. It requires new forms of science that will lead to the knowledge of man.

It is necessary to uplift oneself towards the laws that govern human nature, which are connected to the very laws of the universe, which for millions of years has remained in a condition of harmony.

Education and Democracy

VI/3.   PUBLIC LECTURE, PARIS 1949

Education should not be limited by the democratic ideal or associated with any other ideal which is difficult to define. One wanders far from education when one begins to discuss the exact meaning of the democratic ideal.

Education should be a science and a help to life, a definite and exact study which following the previously discovered laws of life will become something exact and discernible.

Education depends on a belief in the power of the child and on a certainty that the child has within himself the capacity to develop into a being that is far superior to us. He will not only be capable of a better way of living but will be the only person who can show us this.

Therefore at the moment the primary aim of education is: to make everyone conscious of the extreme importance of children. We do not thrust our particular creed or ideal upon them in order that they may grow up to demonstrate it, but we insist that those laws of child life that have been revealed beyond dispute are followed and that research is assisted so that further laws may be revealed.

Education should be regarded as something of such importance that it is not entrusted to just any person, more or less qualified, morally or intellectually; but to persons who are very specially qualified in both these respects.

Education must be organized as all the sciences have had to be in order to get the wonderful results which have been obtained up to the present. It must not be organized as it is in some states in order to display a certain adult attitude but, on the contrary, it should follow the path of other sciences by providing the conditions for study, by setting up the laboratory and the school, then life will display the laws to be followed. Laws of life that have been proved; are they at present scrupulously followed?

Rights of the child! Rights in one sense is a bad word. It appears that the rights of the child might be considered as something just for the child's good. But it is something far greater than that, it is as it were the rights of the soul of humanity, the rights of the greatness and possibility of man to live, a cry that the spirit of man shall be given the possibility to develop to heights such as have already been reached on the material side.

The duties of educators are enormous; it is largely because we have failed to fulfil these duties that the spirit of man has remained where it is. We have been set aside to live near the children. We have had the opportunity to see life unfolding in all its beauty and potentialities, but we have remained blind to it, covered it over with words, stifled it with our preconceived ideas. Now, as it were, the fruit of our labours is turning back on us, we see the results of such an education, and we cannot fail to see that it has been wrong. We must admit that we have been on a wrong path and now turn back to the eternal source of strength, the new beings.[6]

---

[6] The children "sent to us as a rain of souls, as a source of wealth and as a promise, which can always be fulfilled"; cf. introduction to ch. III/2.

MAN'S PLACE IN THE COSMOS

The duty of educators is to insist before the world on the importance of this source of life; to stand together to make a space in which life can grow, where life can have the necessary conditions, and then have the patience and faith to wait for the result: a better order of life, and beings who are capable of living thus.

The rights of educators seem to me to be non-existent, for they are the servants and work as scientists. They must insist that the life they are assisting has the necessary conditions; but beyond that I cannot see that they have any other special rights beyond those of any other adult in the community. Once the general public realizes the sacredness of the task of teaching, and once the standard of assistance given to the children is such that the results in the lives of the adults produced by it is fine and great, then the teachers will be regarded as benefactors to humanity and their advice and assistance will be sought.

One of the obvious causes of the failure of education lies in the training of teachers. Five years to learn to administer the law, as to whether a man shall lose his life; five years to learn to attend to sick bodies; four years to teach children of secondary school age; two years to teach in the elementary school; six months or even no training at all if you are to care for and assist the minds of tiny children. And there life is developing at that most delicate and important stage upon which the welfare of the entire future life depends. It is utterly ridiculous.[7] But do not think that I am suggesting any miraculous effect in 5 years of tiring study and that through it an attitude to life can be developed. All that I am attempting to show is that by present standards the teaching of children is not regarded as anything very important as regards the preparation of the teacher. I insist that there should be a scrupulous moral training for all teachers, and that the idea that specialized intellectual training is necessary only for older pupils is entirely mistaken, or that to be of a patient gentle disposition is all that is necessary for younger children.

---

[7] The development of the education system has partially met Montessori's requirements; with reference to the following passage they are in my opinion still highly relevant.

CHILD, SOCIETY AND THE WORLD

The training of boys and girls now leaving school is not a simple problem. It has to be faced now in a way that is necessarily different from what it will be in the future. Beyond everything I should work to inspire a faith in the greatness of man, the greatness that has been proved by enormous progress. Make clear to them man's place in the world as the improver of the environment of nature, how he has always struggled on, despite being weighed down by so many moral defects. Help them to face up to and understand these moral defects that have crept into all the wonderful things that he has created. They do aspire for something fine, they have a faith in life; but each year that they live in the world they see these institutions of man to be so full of corruption that they attempt to disregard or destroy them. Instead we should help them to see how wonderful is the essence of truth that lies behind them,[8] help them to understand exactly where the moral corruption lies, and then they can do their best to be free of it.[9]

The preparation of the citizen of tomorrow depends entirely on the psychological foundations of man. Men are by nature social beings. They choose to live together, not as a herd but as independently functioning beings who associate together. This instinct is displayed by very young children who, as soon as they have worked as independent beings, associate with others. This desire to associate is something so strong that it is possible that some of the errors of adult society are due only to the fact that education of young children has aimed so much at frustrating this desire, and then when the disastrous results were seen many artificial remedies were applied in the hopes of curing the ill caused.

Again, to speak of a democratic school community seems to be asking for misunderstanding. It is a community of children, a community of future men and women, real men and women, who, when they have once been allowed to develop no one will doubt are real men and women. They are going to live in the

---

[8] In the historical achievements of the human race.

[9] This "enlightening" aspect of the Montessori method as a necessary condition for the protection of young people against radical social "divergence" is in my mind highly relevant.

world, therefore they must have contact with it and understand it before they enter it. Life in the adult world is only another phase of life, the last phase of the many that have led up to it. In all the other phases one prepared for the next phase before entering it. Here also there must be real and definite preparation, so that when they enter the social life of the adult they can master the mechanisms that control it. In themselves the mechanisms of social life are quite rational, but because so few people understand them the mechanisms now control the lives of men. Children must experience social life through living, through experience, before they enter it with all the many forms of mechanisms that control it.[10]

The subjects of instruction can definitely contribute to an understanding of these mechanisms. For the children must understand the present, the economic and political factors controlling the world. To imagine, as is sometimes done, that this can be given in the last years at school is ludicrous. The facts, the plain facts, as for instance the distribution of steel in the world, who owns and controls it, is study fit for very young children.[11] The older children[12] need and desire to know the effects that such facts have had and will continue to have. They need to have the facts at their disposal and from that work out for themselves what must be the controlling influences. The history of the present is enormously important, and not only the present but its roots in the past through which much of the present can be understood. History of the past should be taught with this view in mind, as the explanation of the present. Give also to these children a vivid picture of the struggle and greatness of man's progress, show that he has moved on step by step; let them realize the greatness of man's present position, that he has mastered the external elements. Only the progress of his own soul has been neglected and that is because the child, who holds within himself the possibility of progress in the soul, has up till the present been regarded as the son of man rather

---

[10] Compare Montessori's suggestions for a residential school in the country in: *From Childhood to Adolescence*, New York, Schocken, 1976.

[11] Those aged between 6 and 12.

[12] From 12 to 18 years; see notes 10 and Ch. VI/4.

than the father of man, an infinitely superior being to his teachers.[13]

Cosmic Education

VI/4.   LECTURE, INDIA 1946

To give an idea of what we mean by Cosmic Education it is necessary to touch upon the background of the question, i.e., the cosmic theory. This recognizes in all creation a unifying plan upon which depend not only the different forms of living beings, but also the evolution of the earth itself. This idea, although it includes the foundation of evolution theory, differs upon the causes and the finality of the progressive changes of the species. The progress of life through its struggles and its defences is not due to change. Life progresses according to a cosmic plan and the purpose of life is not to achieve perfection along an unlimited line of progress but to exercise influence and to achieve a definite aim upon the environment. Geology has long shown the close relation between life and earth and has considered the life which cloaks the whole surface of the earth as the "biosphere" necessary to the building up of the earth. In fact, most rocks, the mountains, the islands, and even continents have been built by animals, especially by the corals. The purity of sea water and the constancy of its composition – which is so necessary to the life of the fishes and molluscs which live in the ocean – is due to the continuous work of purification carried on by the corals, the shellfishes, and by some unicellular animals whose remains cover the bottom of the oceans and which later on are transformed into marbles, chalks and rocks. The purity of the air and the unchanging quantity of oxygen which renders the air breathable to all land animals is due to vegetable life, and especially to the trees that first appeared upon the earth when it arose from the waters, so that the earth and the water form a constructive unit. It was recently proved on observing the functions of the animals that their behaviour,

---

[13] The saying "the child is the father of the man" probably comes originally from the poet Wordsworth (1770–1850) whom Montessori occasionally quotes.

their individual mode of acting in the environment has the purpose not only of maintaining themselves, but above all, of carrying a specific item in the complex task of the upkeep of the earth and of maintaining harmony on it. To realize this one need only think of the first brilliant example given by Darwin concerning the close collaboration between flowering plants and insects. The insect which goes to seek nourishment in the flower of the plant carries out unconsciously an altruistic task, the pollination of the flowers. He ensures in this way the crossing and the survival of the plants. Similarly all other animals by the process of feeding themselves or seeking food carry out a "cosmic" task which contributes to keep nature in a harmonious state of purity. Each kind works for the whole and upon the work of each depends the possibility of the life of the whole. These cosmic tasks have been wisely distributed among all the behaviour which urges it irresistibly to some task which is useful for the community. Ecology is a new science which studies these correlations. When one observes the generality of this contribution one cannot but wonder about Man. Is Humanity the only parasite who lives among useless struggles and immense work merely to keep itself living? Is it possible that only Man spends his brief span of life suffering in this terrestrial world to no purpose? This cannot be so. It is evident that the cosmic theory must include also man among the agents of creation. We must observe this behaviour in order to find out what are his essential functions which contribute to the upkeep and the development of the earth. It immediately springs to the eye that man exerts a "modifying function" upon nature. From the beginning of time he worked (and he continues at first sight to do so) for his own benefit, but living upon the earth he leaves a trace of his existence and enchanted path. Wherever man passed the flowers became more beautiful, the plants richer, the jungles became forests and the waters were distributed. Even what was buried in the earth for millions of years – such as coal – came back to the surface, so returning to the atmosphere its essential elements; the energies which were unexploited in the Ether were utilized; chemical substances which were in earth were used for new compositions. Even the precious stones that had formed in the aeons of time came to shine in the light of the external world. Animals were better distributed over the surface of the earth, and the earth itself that once had as animal constructions only beehives, the towers of termites, and the nests of birds, covered itself with the monuments created by the genius of man.

And man himself, in building that which we call civilization, multiplied his powers to the point that he overcame all the limitations of nature and rose above the conditions that were his at the moment of his first appearance upon the earth. He to whom nature had given only two feet to walk upon, can today cross the earth by mechanical means which transport him from one end to the other, passing through continents as well as oceans and even through the wide spaces of the atmosphere. Human intelligence has become almost all-powerful and today has arrived at a point where it can dominate the energies of the world and penetrate the most intimate secrets of life.

Therefore, instead of being a parasite, he is the one who not only enjoys the environment, but is the most active of the agents who are destined to modify and perfect it. His energy is almost all-powerful and through his endeavours he has so transformed himself as to become able to realize the miracles of a new creation. If we compare conditions of the earth before his appearance to the earth as we know it today we get an idea of the power of humanity as a cosmic agent. Yet the span of the existence of humanity when compared to the length of the geological epochs shows humanity to be so young as to enable us to say that it is only at the beginning of its cosmic task. This task seems to be unlimited and to lead to supernatural and divine powers. The intelligence and the sentiments of mankind have evolved through its creative cosmic task. What we have today is the realization of what was felt by intuition in the religions of thousands of years ago. There is a series of very ancient writings which have been collected in a book called "Ahinahita" and which showed Man the path by which to reach God. This path is not of meditation nor is it one of inquiry into the spiritual reason of things, but "to redeem the earth and to transform the deserts into Paradise". It is through this work which is as constant as a function, "the function of Man", that humanity will grow up to the point of approaching the understanding of God. (These writings which originated in Tibet are considered by Max Müller[14] as the foundation of all the ancient religions of Persia and India.)

But while carrying out this long task where Man acts as the cosmic agent who refines and perfects the creations of nature, humanity remained, as did all the other animals, unconscious of having a cosmic task in creation. It thought of living for its own good, only evolving upon the basis of its own defences and on its own efforts towards conquest, and even now continues to ask itself what is the purpose of life of man upon the earth, what is the meaning of his laborious pilgrimage? Man ponders over the unique uselessness of his efforts at conquest and upon the hard necessity of his defences, and he concludes that everything is a passing illusion. This shows that he is unaware of his task, in the same way as the corals live without being conscious that they are building islands and continents.

This vision leaves one to reconsider prehistory and the history of man from a fresh viewpoint which affords the key to understanding human society better. Men first formed into separate groups (tribes and nations), elaborating locally different elements of civilization (cosmic task) destined to mix and join together as the atoms do when they join according to their own combinations to construct new and more complex substances. And finally, in the present epoch, the union of all humanity seems to have been reached unconsciously, for today man exchanges not only the produce of his material activity but also the thoughts, the discoveries, and all the products that arise from the work of pure intelligence. One thing is very clear today: that humanity is effectively united. Yet this union was not a conscious task, a conscious aim. On the contrary, men have remained so unconscious of the fact that the evidence of the union has been realized more under the form of the threat of destruction than under the guise of a superb triumph of creation.

One thing still evades the intelligence of humanity and that is the consciouness of their terrestrial destiny and of the fact that the whole of humanity is so intimately united that it forms but

---

[14] F(riedrich) Max Müller (1823–1900), philologist and expert in Sanskrit, founder of the study of comparative religions.

one organized energy. The revolutionary movements of our days are a sign of the great crisis from which "the Universal Consciousness" of humanity is about to be born.

From the extreme dangers of our days the vision is born of the necessity that men should with their conscious will and with their sentiment, seek to find the "adaptation" to present conditions, thus forming one universal harmonious society. This is the aspiration to which today humanity clings, urged by the supreme appeal of seeking its own salvation. But how to attain this if not through a "direct preparation" of the new generation, i.e., through education?

Man was urged almost exclusively to carry out his cosmic mission and in doing so he forgot himself. Today he is not "prepared" to dominate the environment which is composed of a "supra-nature"[15] created upon the earth by himself. He depends blindly and unconsciously upon circumstances that he himself prepared when he was unconscious of his finalities upon the earth. Men did not take care of humanity. Its growth was neglected and left to chance and thus remained inferior in development to the development of the environment in which he lives. He is without orientation and without control over his own creation. The first step in education, and the most urgent one, is to direct care and attention to human individuality which must be studied and known in its psychic side as nature came to be known through the minutely detailed study of biology. The hour has come in which a universal appeal sounds directed towards humanity. Science first studied life in general; it must now study the life of Man. Psychology is a newborn science which is about to attract upon itself the most lively interest. It tends immediately not only to know the psychology of man from birth itself but to modify man as nature itself was modified. This modification of man is felt not as a desire towards the new form of knowledge but as an immediate necessity upon which depends the very safety of humanity. Men are ignorant, unconscious and unoriented in their practical behaviour, even the most eminent ones who direct the faith of humanity. It is

---

[15] Montessori wanted to ensure that her term "supra-nature" was clearly differentiated from the theological concept of the "supernatural".

necessary to help the human individual from birth to develop all the latent energies, to acquire a clearer intelligence, a stronger character, a new and freer form of consciousness capable of understanding the totality of human needs. Then in the same way as biology showed the fashion of controlling life, of making use of its hidden energies and thus creating new flowers and new fruits that were unknown in crude nature, only then can a new man and a more perfect one be created in future generations. Human life and the child can no longer remain unknown and left to themselves, restricted by the bounds of old prejudices which limit and deform its expansion. The plan of an education which will give salvation must be based upon the laws that govern human growth and must realize all the potential energies which are latent in man. When the problem is faced by taking into consideration the roots of individuality, it is possible to find an easier and a clearer path along which to conduct the new generations, free and imbued with new vigour towards the acquisition of a new orientation of consciousness, and towards the harmonious union of all mankind. In other words, it is through a childhood modified and freed from the ties of unconsciousness, of weakness, of psychic deviations and of ignorance, that it is possible to act by giving a new form of intellectual culture and by cultivating new sentiments for humanity. It is this later part, culture, that which represents the study to be carried out in the schools, the universal syllabus that can unite the mind and the consciousness of all men in one harmony, that we intend by "Cosmic Education".

This education must take its departure and spread from one centre, the cosmic plan of creation. In this concern, all that has developed during the different civilizations achieved by different groups is a preparation for the great and supreme triumph of the human agent who has already reached dominion over all things and who must now find dominion over himself. It has prepared a united and all-powerful energy in a union which, though unconscious, is real and which consists of all human individuals in one organized body.

In the universal syllabus of studies to which the new generations must apply themselves, all the items of culture must be concerned as different aspects of the knowledge of the world and the cosmos. Astronomy, geography, geology, biology, physics, chemistry are but details of one whole. It is their relation to one another that urges interest from a centre towards its ramifications. There is besides this the other part which concerns the directing of the consciousness towards humanity. The cosmic construction of human society must be the core of the study of history and sociology. How can we appreciate humanity if we do not consider first of all its merits, its creative efforts, its obedience to cosmic laws that have unconsciously urged society towards an effective union that today unites the whole of humanity in one vital aspect?

It is necessary that the new generations realize that in this union every man is dependent on other men and each must contribute to the existence of all. We no longer depend directly upon nature, but on all that man produces in different parts of the world and is put at the disposal of all through mutual exchange. For our material life we depend upon the working man, on him who produces for us and for all the necessities of life. And we depend also upon the intellectual workers for every item of progress which renders our life easier and richer. An infinite number of heroes have struggled to render "knowledge" possible. All that we study today depends upon some individual discovery no matter how great or how small. There is no detail of a geographical map which is not based on the effort and heroism of explorers who for the most part remain unknown. The alphabet, writing, mathematics, printing, and everything that forms the means of our culture are due to a series of efforts of individuals whose names in the majority of cases are forgotten. It is to man, always to man, that is due all that comes to enrich the mind and to facilitate life.

An ardent admiration towards this prodigious humanity must be the fundamental sentiment of the new generations. They must feel the pride and privilege of belonging to humanity. Man must appear as a sacred being of creation and as the greatest marvel of nature and the sentiment of "gratitude and love" for all the advantages that we enjoy in life must be aroused with every step that is taken in the field of culture. No object must be made use of without the thought that some unknown man produced it. The morsel of bread, the handful of rice, the dress, the house, the road, the means of transportation, everything was given to us by men. Their effort and their sacrifice for us must always be present in our consciousness. The coal that gives us warmth was torn from the bowels of the earth by men who consecrated their life to this arduous and dangerous task. Everything is found, built, invented and transported by man.

Who in the new generations will dare to destroy man, the sacred being who provides for our needs as would a prodigious mother? To offend humanity is to be blindly and barbarously ignorant. From this education must arise the persuasion that mutual help among men is the most direct form of universal defence. The need or the inferiority of a people are a real danger for the whole of humanity and it is in the interests of all to find the means to satisfy those needs and to uplift men from their state of inferiority. This has been understood in the physical field, where the unhygienic condition of any one spot is a danger also for the people who enjoy perfect hygiene conditions and it has been found that the best way of assuring one's own health is to better those conditions. Human society must reach a level of average welfare where the necessities of life can be satisfied for all people.

This concept resembles that of some religions. Without doubt, the cosmic concept has an affinity with the "Unity of God the Creator", recognized in many religions. Unity among men as well as help for the weak form part of the Christian spirit and of that of other religions. These two concepts answer to every lofty religious institution. But that which stands out in the cosmic theory is not only the utility of giving help to man, but the justice which must be rendered to humanity for its merits and the recognition of the fact that we owe all to its efforts. In religions, by contrast, everything which is good and which we enjoy, is attributed to the mercy of God. In social life, however, much of what we enjoy must be laid to the credit of the work of man. We might repeat here "Give unto God that which is God's and unto Man that which is Man's." It is necessary to arouse that religious sentiment of gratitude that was given to God also towards man. Religious respect for sacred humanity as the effective dispenser of God's mercy must be aroused in the coming generations. And offence to human life must be felt as a sacrilege. If this is not so, the "Curse of God" will visit us again and again in the shape of disastrous wars for having disregarded man, the sacred provider of the common wellbeing of us all.

Select Bibliography

Books by Maria Montessori (arranged chronologically by original year of publication)

The Discovery of the Child (Oxford, England: Clio Press, 1988 [First published in English translation as *The Montessori Method*, New York: F.A. Stokes, 1912]).

Dr. Montessori's Own Handbook (London: Heinemann, 1914).

The Advanced Montessori Method (Science Pedagogy as Applied to the Education of Children from Seven to Eleven Years):
Vol. I. Spontaneous Activity in Education (London: Heinemann, 1918).
Vol. II. The Montessori Elementary Material (London: Heinemann, 1918).

The Child in the Church (London: Sands, 1929).

Peace and Education (Geneva: International Bureau of Education, 1932).

The Secret of Childhood (New York: Ballantine Books [First published London, New York, Toronto: Longmans 1936]).

Education for a New World (Oxford, England: Clio Press 1989 [First published Adyar, Madras: Kalakshetra, 1946]).

To Educate the Human Potential (Oxford, England, Clio Press 1989 [First published Adyar, Madras: Kalakshetra, 1948]).

The Discovery of the Child (Revised and enlarged edition of *The Montessori Method*, Oxford, England: Clio Press, 1988 [First published Adyar, Madras: Kalakshetra, 1948]).

The Absorbent Mind (Oxford, England: Clio Press, 1988 [First published Adyar, Madras: Theosophical Publishing, 1949]).

The Child in the Family (Oxford, England: 1989 [First published London: Pan, 1975]).

From Childhood to Adolescence (New York: Schocken, 1976 [First published 1948]).

Childhood Education (New York: Meridian, 1975).

Books about Maria Montessori (arranged chronologically by original year of publication)

Maccheroni, Anna Maria. *A True Romance: Dr. Maria Montessori as I Knew Her* (Edinburgh: 1947).

SELECT BIBLIOGRAPHY

Standing, Edwin Mortimer. *Maria Montessori: Her Life and Work* (London: 1947).

MacCormick Rambusch, Nancy. *Learning how to Learn: An American Approach to Montessori* (Baltimore: 1962).

McVicker Hunt, J. *Revisiting Montessori*. In: *The Montessori Method by Maria Montessori* (New York: 1964, xi–xxxix).

Cavalletti, Sofia/Gobbi, Gianna. *Teaching Doctrine and Liturgy* (New York: 1964 2nd edn).

Smardridge, Norah. *The Light Within* (New York: 1965).

Standing, Edwin Mortimer. *The Montessori Revolution in Education* (New York: 1967).

Berger, B. *A Longitudinal Investigation of Montessori and Traditional Prekindergarten Training with Innercity Children: a Comparative Assessment of Learning Outcomes* (New York: 1969).

Gitter, Lena L. *Montessori's Legacy to Children* (Washington: 1970).

Orem, R.C. *Montessori and the Special Child: An Application of Montessori Principles to Educating the Handicapped, the Disadvantaged and Other Children out of the Norm* (New York: 1970).

Orem, R.C./Stevens, George L. *American Montessori Manual: Principles, Applications, Terms* (Johnstown, Pennsylvania: 1970).

Orem, R.C. *Montessori Today* (New York: 1971).

Lillard, P. Polk. *Montessori: A Modern Approach* (New York: 1972).

Fleege, Virginia B. *Montessori Index* (Oak Park, Illinois: 1974 2nd edn).

Miller, Jean K. *The Montessori Elementary School and its Curriculum* (Cleveland, Ohio: 1974).

Kramer, Rita. *Maria Montessori: A Biography* (New York: 1976).

Montessori, Mario M., Jr. *Education for Human Development* (New York: 1977).

Orem, R.C./Foster Coburn, Marjorie. *Montessori: Prescription for Children with Learning Disabilities* (New York: 1978).

APPENDIX: LIST OF SOURCES

Order in	Page	Title in text	Title in original	Original language	Circumstances of origin	Date	Translator from Italian	Transcription notes by	Archive no. or document/vol.	Notes
I/1	4	When your child knows better than you	When your child knows better than you	English	unknown	c. 1930	unknown	unknown	Baarn C 12	Wrongly identified as the text 'Le due vite' in the archive manuscript
I/2	6	Let your child keep his secret	Let your child keep his secret	English	unknown	c. 1930	unknown	unknown	Baarn C 9	Presumably the same manuscript producer as I/1 (from cover details)
I/3	9	"Maturity theory"?	Excerpt from: Broadcast by Dr Maria Montessori	English (obviously broadcast in English)	Radio interview with Miss Sperry	15.4.50	Mr Mario Montessori Sr	from the original Italian manuscript by Maria Montessori (not traced)	Baarn R 3	Interview with 'World Radio'
II/1	12	Concentration and the teacher	untitled Lecture 32	English	International Montessori Course London 1946	10.12.46	Mr Mario Montessori Sr	Miss Homfray and Miss Child	Lectures, held by Dr Maria Montessori during a Montessori Training Course London 1946	Photocopy

II/2	18	Rules for the teacher of young children in the "Children's House"	Excerpt from: L'adulto (Parte pratica, p. 54–5)	Italian	International Montessori Course Barcelona 1933	1933		Signora Lina Olivero (notes in the original language of the lecture)	M. Montessori XVIII. Corso Internazionale Note sul Lavoro Practico, Barcelona, 1933	Translation for non-Italian-speaking course members by various translation teams
III/1	21	On social education	untitled Lecture 33	English	International Montessori Course London 1946	11.12.46	Mr Mario Montessori Sr	Miss Homfray and Miss Child	See II/1	See II/1
III/2 (a)	30	On religious education (a)	untitled	English	Convent Parallel Course (to the 22nd International Montessori Course) London 1937	3.3.37	A.M. Maccheroni	unknown	Baarn R 8	Location: Convent of the Assumption, Kensington Square, London
(b)	35	On religious education (b)	untitled Lecture 28	English	International Montessori Course London 1946	29.11.46	Mr Mario Montessori Sr	Miss Homfray and Miss Child	See II/1	See II/1
III/3	44	On fantasy and fairy tales	untitled Lecture 26	English	International Montessori Course London 1946	26.11.46	Mr Mario Montessori Sr	Miss Homfray and Miss Child	See II/1	See II/1
III/4	51	The "lesson of silence"	Leçon de silence (XXIV. Conference)	French	1st Montessori training course in Laren, Netherlands 1938/39	18.11.38	Lecture by Maria Montessori in French	Mr Joosten and Miss Paolini	Dssa Maria Montessori, 1° Corso del Montessori Training Centre Laren, Netherlands 1938/39	Continued in Lecture XXVII (25.11.38). Translated for the Dutch audience by Mevr. R. Joosten

									Included as an appendix to: Dr Montessori's Lectures to 7th Indian Montessori Training Course, Karachi	Contains explanatory notes on 'some interesting dates'
IV/1	61	On the principles of the Montessori School	untitled Lecture by Dr Maria Montessori	English	Indian Montessori Course 1942 Adyar, Madras	30.1.42	Mr Mario Montessori Sr	unknown		
V/1 (a)	72	Children, teachers and society	untitled Lecture 29	English	International Montessori Course London 1946	3.12.46	Mr Mario Montessori Sr	Miss Homfray and Miss Child	See II/1	See II/1
(b)	75	Children, teachers and society	untitled Lecture 30	English	International Montessori Course London 1946	4.12.46	Mr Mario Montessori Sr	Miss Homfray and Miss Child	See II/1	See II/1
V/2	81	Protection against exploitation of children	untitled (excerpt)	English	Lectures at the University of Madras, 2–8 Feb. 1940	8.2.40	Mr Mario Montessori Sr	unknown	Dr Maria Montessori, Lectures delivered at University of Madras, 2–8 Feb. 1940	From a short series of lectures
V/3	83	Work as an anthropological necessity	untitled (excerpt)	English	Lectures at the University of Madras, 2–8 Feb. 1940	8.2.40	see V/2	see V/2	see V/2	see V/2

								Signorina Guidi (notes in the original language of the lecture)	Lectures Dr Montessori, Course Rome (April–June 1951)	
V/4	87	On the schooling of young people	Prima conferenza sull' adolescenza	Italian	Montessori Course, Rome 1951	April–June 1951				
VI/1	95	Man's place in creation	untitled	English	Individual lectures at a convent in London, 1935	13.9. 35	A.M. Maccheroni	unknown	Lecture given by Dr Montessori at the convent on 13 Sept. 1935 — Baarn R 7	On the occasion of a training course in London: Location: Convent of the Assumption, Kensington Square, London
VI/2	99	Communism and peace	Communism and peace	English	Probably originated in Laren, Netherlands	end of 1930s	Mr Mario Montessori Sr	based on the original manuscript by Maria Montessori (cannot be traced)	Baarn C 19	Probably only private notes; (many notes were lost in 1940 with the German invasion)
VI/3	101	Education and democracy	Notes for the Paris Conference 'Teachers and the realization of the democratic ideal'	English	Public lecture in Paris	1949	Mr Mario Montessori Sr	based on an original Italian manuscript by Maria Montessori (not traced)	Baarn D 14	Probably in note form
VI/4	106	Cosmic education	Cosmic education	English	Opening address at the 1st All-Indian Montessori Congress in Pilani	1.1.46 (Date of typing of manuscript)	Mr Mario Montessori Sr	unknown	Baarn C 21	Date of speech probably Dec. 1945 (handwritten note on typed manuscript)

INDEX

INDEX

INDEX

INDEX

INDEX

religion, religious 86, 98, 108–9, 113
religious education 28–42, 93
repeat, repetition 80
repression 3, 12, 25, 77–8, 79, 100
research 74
respect 19, 21, 22, 23, 113
responsibility 6, 20, 94
restlessness 5
revelation 39, 54
revolution, revolutionary 71, 100, 101, 110
Ridgway, L. 60
right moment, the 61
rights 83, 101, 102 *see also* human rights
Röhrs, H. 43
Rome, Roman 66, 67, 71, 87, 89
Roncalli, Cardinal 29
rote learning 38, 48–9
ruin 71
rules 18, 72

sacrilege 113
salvation 110, 111
San Lorenzo 11
Scheid, P. viii, 20, 43, 93
Schmutzler, H. J. 43
school age 3
school society/life 22, 104
schooling 87–92
schools 3, 75 *see also* elementary; ordinary; secondary (schools)
Schulz-Benesch, G. viii, 3, 21, 28, 29, 30, 43, 51, 60
science, scientist, scientific 93, 98, 100, 110
secondary schools 71, 103
secrets 6–9, 96
    psychic 100
secret(s) of life 97, 108
security 18, 41, 99
self-discipline 5, 8
self-preservation 84
senses, sensory period 32, 34, 35
sensibility 34, 37
sensitive, sensitivity 13, 56
sentiment(s) 108, 110, 111
sermon, preaching 40, 75, 82
serve 86–7, 99

silence 19, 23, 33, 50–8, 69
singing 13, 17, 64
single (one) nation 71, 93 *see also* Nazione unica
slavery, tyranny 89–90, 92
sloth 85
social activity 24
social conditions 70, 110
social discipline 24
social education 20–8, 72, 74
social environment 22
social life 22, 24, 72, 73, 105, 113
social needs 100
social problems 83
social question 81
social relationships 21
social sense 22
social sentiment 25
social tensions 71
socialist, socialism 82
society 22, 27, 72–4, 75, 76, 82, 87, 109, 112
society by cohesion 22, 24, 27
sociology 112
soft words 19 *see also* sweet words
soul 14, 19, 36, 39, 40, 42, 75, 85, 93–4, 98, 105
Speck, J. 59
speech *see* spoken language
Sperry, Miss 9
spirit 95–6
spiritual 13, 19, 108
    atmosphere 37
spiritual development 36, 57
spoken language, speech 9, 44–5
spontaneous 22
    discipline 23, 56
Spranger, E. 43
state monopoly 60
state schools 92 *see also* ordinary schools
Steggemann, R. 51
stillness 54
stories 17, 34 *see also* fairy tales
study 87, 89, 92
sub-conscious 9, 21, 37, 90
subjugation 91
submissiveness, submission 45
subtle 56

125